Give me shelter

compiled by

Michael Rosen

B H

ACKNOWLEDGEMENTS

The publishers would like to thank the following:

All at Shelter for their help during the compiling of the book, especially Fiona Hesseldon, Sheila McKechnie, Jessica Morris and Debbie Nelson.

Paul Miller would like to thank the following people who so kindly allowed him to photograph them: Einstein, Simon, Mark, Tony, Gandalf, Dave and Donna, John and Natasha, Simon, Stewart Walsh and all at the Homeless People's Street Theatre, Grace, Yorkie, Lizzie, Keesha, Baz, Paul, Sue, Dave and Harry, Tony, Mick and Nick, Jock, Smurf, Tommy, Kelly, Jools, Patience, The London Connection Football Team, Keisha, Kathy, Paul, John, Sharon, Tom, Kevin, Sky, Denise, Jackie and many others whose names I don't know.

Peter Butler for long hours in the darkroom.

We would also like to thank the following organizations for their assistance: Alone in London, Centrepoint — Vauxhall, Centrepoint — Soho, The Squatters Advisory Service,
Metropolitan Police — Bow Street, and especially all the staff and users at The London Connection, Les Milner and St Basil's Centre, Birmingham, St Botolph's Crypt.

Also Dave Laws, Andrew Leach for suggestions, and John Lilley for last minute checking.

Grateful thanks for the following permissions: Bronski Music Ltd. for permission to use *Smalltown Boy © 1988 Bronski Music Ltd.*, administered by Zomba Music Publishers Ltd/Jesse Musique Ltd. Pogue Music Ltd and Perfect Music Ltd. for permission to use *The Old Main Drag*, The Pogues.© 1985 Pogue Music Ltd./Perfect Music Ltd. All rights reserved. Andrew Wiard for kind permission to reprint his photographs on the back cover. And *The Independent* newspaper for permission to reprint Jack O'Sullivan's report.

And the following suppliers: Horsells and Gibbons JCR LTD for supplying plates and ink, Fineblade cartridge paper supplied by Townsend Hook, Mac Attack Bureau, London and printing by Scotprint Ltd.

Special thanks are due to Ness Wood for getting the book designed on time, against all odds. Alison Ritchie for all her editorial input and for keeping a panic-stricken Editor going with witty solace . . . Stephen Gaymer for being a wizz on the Apple Mac! All of them for working through the night to get the book finished, Milly Molly Mandy Sherliker for the tea and pizza, and Timmy for keeping quiet.

Alison and Ness would like to thank A.J. for pulling them and the book together.

Text design by Ness Wood.
Cover designed by Senate Design Ltd.
All rights reserved.
First published in 1991 by The Bodley Head Children's Books
an imprint of The Random Century Group Ltd 20 Vauxhall Bridge Road, London SWIV 2SA
Printed and bound by Scotprint Ltd.

A catalogue record for this book is available from
the British Library
ISBN 0 370 31613 4

CONTENTS

ILLUSTRATIONS

Steve Bell 31

Marylou North 39

Andrezej Krauze 56, 61, 63, 69

John Bently 71, 106, 157

Posy Simmonds 97

Ros Asquith 105

Clara Vulliamy 130

Paul Thomas 145, 169

David Huggins 159

Maggie Ling 170

Bill Tidy 171

David Haldane 172

Tony Husband 173

Photographs by Paul Miller

PREFACE
MICHAEL ROSEN

I've never been homeless. This means that the young people I
see in the corridors of the London Underground, or begging
along the cinema queues are, in a true sense, strangers. So,
like many others, I scan their faces for an explanation. Why are
they here? But no explanations come. As with the photos in
this book, all I see is a terrible normality — people who could
be friends, relations, people I know.

Shelter — the National Campaign for homeless people— was
set up in 1966, and as we move into the nineties, we mark 25
years of their campaign to secure decent and affordable
housing as a right for all. Their relentless battle continues
against the odds as the situation worsens with a record number
of homeless people in Britain this year.

Indeed, in 1973, a book was published called 'The House that
Jack Built — Poems for Shelter'. I have been re-reading it,
hoping that I might come across a poem suitable for this
collection. No chance. True, the poems were angry, but the
trouble was they were all about housing — you know — homes.
Nearly twenty years later and we've moved on. The rain is still
running down the walls of multi-occupied blocks but now it's
blowing on to the sleeping bags underneath the arches too.

Anyone who writes words or makes images hopes that people
will stop for a moment and take note. This book is no
exception, but this time those whose situation has inspired the
words and images will also be hoping that people will stop for a
moment and take note.

FOREWORD

'I think we can make it unnecessary for people to sleep rough' said Sir George Young, Minister for Housing, last year.

If only it was unnecessary. . . None of us like seeing 16-year-olds bedding down in shop doorways, queuing up for hostel places, suffering frostbite and hypothermia. But that is the reality.

How can we live in a society that cares so little for its young that they have to beg in order to survive? How many more reports, campaigns, meetings with ministers, letters and petitions have to happen before the crisis facing young people is dealt with?

Set up in 1966, Shelter has been working for change for 25 years. It is a damning indictment of our current housing system that we are now having to campaign for people who weren't even born when Shelter was started. We would prefer not to have to be here, yet there remains a pressing need for Shelter: to provide direct help for those in need and to argue for more homes that people can afford.

Homelessness in Britain is not the result of a national disaster like a flood or a famine. This is still a rich country. Homelessness is primarily a failure of the housing system. We simply don't have enough housing that people can afford. When there is a shortage of over a million homes it is not hard to work out who will lose: those with the least ability to pay.

Young people without any income come pretty near the end of the queue. Many are without income because they can't get a job. And young unemployed people receive less benefit than those over 25. There are too few jobs to go round, and even for those who can find work, wages are often far too low to meet rents, since the cost of housing has risen sharply in recent years. This has led to record increases in youth homelessness. Shelter estimates that 156,000 young people have experienced

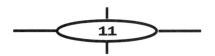

homelessness at some stage this year.

Many young unemployed people are caught up in a vicious Catch 22 situation whereby no job means no home, and being homeless makes applying for jobs and persuading potential employers of your suitability often impossible. These problems are compounded by cuts in young people's state benefits, introduced in September 1988. Most 16-to 18-year- olds not on a Youth Training scheme find they are excluded from any Income Support. The end result is clear: young people literally living on the streets, begging for change.

But the plight of young homeless people is also a symptom of a much wider malaise in our housing system. Since the mid-seventies Britain has had a love affair with owner occupation and a growing dislike of social housing in any form. It has been difficult at times to decide whether politicians have simply gone with the grain of public opinion or created it. A bit of both is probably the case.

The benefits of owner occupation—financial gain, security, control, choice — have been obvious to those in middle income secure jobs. But not everyone is in a secure job. The consequences of pushing more and more people into buying as other forms of housing, private renting, council housing and housing associations become less available, is becoming all too obvious. This year there will be more people having their homes repossessed because they cannot afford the mortgage than there is rented housing for them to go to.

Shelter has been raising these issues since its birth 25 years ago. And we continue to pose the crucial questions we asked at the start: how can we best meet housing need? How can housing be made affordable to the poorest sections of our society?

In our 25th anniversary year, we are campaigning around the theme 'Building For The Future', because we want to look ahead to see how we are going to house our children; how we are going to stop today's crisis becoming tomorrow's nightmare.

And we will continue giving free, expert advice and assistance to those in

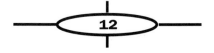

desperate housing need. Shelter's nationwide network of more than 25 housing aid centres means we can offer impartial and confidential advice to more than 35,000 people every year. Shelter's advisers are kept up to date on the complexities of housing law through our in-depth training courses. Good advice can prevent people becoming homeless. And through our contact with people experiencing housing problems we are able to pin-point difficulties and press for change.

This book of stories, poems, photographs and illustrations, however, reminds us all that behind every cold statistic there are real people suffering real hardship.

'Give Me Shelter' is not a celebration of Shelter's anniversary. It is a hard reminder of why we exist. It will help us to raise money for our work. It may even make you think.

This cannot go on.

Sheila McKechnie

Sheila McKechnie
Director of Shelter
October 1991

HUNGERFORD BRIDGE

KATIE CAMPBELL

Hunger.

Please sir.

Can you spare . . . Can you ford it. Can you afford . . .

Please sir.

Dirty layabouts, sorry Darling.

These walkways; next time we'll bring the car.

Hey man got any

change?

Change. Change. They've got to do something about this. I mean

this is disgusting, atrocious. This is our Capital City.

En route to one of the

Great Cultural Treasures and this . . .

Fuckit man I'm starvin'

Darling haven't you . . .

Don't bother, they'll simply drink it away.

He doesn't even have

A place to stay. A cup of tea.

He's shivering.

It's all part of the act.

Please sir.

Look at that one down the way, with his dog. Now that's what I

call Cheap Emotion. Exploitation.

Like those gypsies in the tube with their babies.

Should be forbidden.

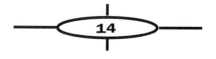

Children should be in school, playgrounds, off the street.

And this animal. Cruelty. Should be reported.

Enough for a tin of dog food, that's all . . .

I'd give it him if I thought he'd use it to feed the dog.

You can't be sure though . . . Dog probably forages for himself.

Rubbish bags. Scattering the muck all over the street for people

to trip on. No way.

Too bad. It's a beautiful creature. Perhaps he'll sell it.

Golden goose. Forget it. Hurry Darling, we'll be late.

Please sir.

Oh disgusting. Imagine cuddling next to the creature like that.

It's so unhygienic.

Probably for warmth.

But the fleas. What about fleas and the dirt?

The dog looks cleaner than the man.

Got any spare change?

What's this city . . .

Change of government that's what . . .

Look Darling there's two of them under that thing, blanket, rug.

Yuk it stinks.

Please. Hurry now Darling, don't trip on that stuff.

Can't we give him something?

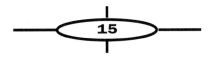

How about a cigarette?

I'd rather a pound for a cup of tea.

Ungrateful creatures.

Unhealthy to smoke, but if you've got a spare sandwich

(smoked salmon perhaps? wild pheasant? partridge?)

Cigarette?

No. I don't smoke, it's unhealthy, didn't you know.

Numbs the hunger.

Get something to eat.

hunger

Can you spare a . . .
Hurry Darling, it will start without us.

Look at the lights, see St Brides over there behind that ghastly modern carbunkle. St Brides, layered like a wedding cake, my favourite spire in the city . . . view so obscured with these building cranes. Should be stopped. All this development. Ruining the . . .

This is my favourite place in the whole world. I only bring special . . .
It used to be special before . . .
Please sir, can you . . .
Ruining the city this trash. Should be swept away. We live in a welfare . . . go on the dole . . . nobody needs to . . . healthy and young.

Please sir.
No, I haven't got anything.
Nothing to give . . .
But Darling I saw you gave to that man with the flute the wand the performing cats the cards the stilts the balloons the big nose . . .
Yes, but that's entertainment.
Giss a . . .
Something for nothing that's what they want. Well life's not like that. They won't get it from me; that's false charity, giving them unrealistic ideas. I'm being cruel to be kind.

I can wiggle my ears. I can make shadow puppets against the bridge after dark. Anything more energetic is tough these days on my calorie count. One Big Mac last night. Half a hot dog this morning. I can sing for my supper, sing like a jungle, howl like

IN 1988 THE GOVERNMENT STOPPED PROVIDING INCOME SUPPORT FOR MOST 16 AND 17 YEAR OLDS.

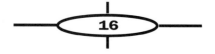

the moon with her blanket of ice and the trains hurrying past to
rock me all night.

In the olden days it was work or starve, you didn't have these . . .
pests . . . like this: vagrants, vermin — worse:
Please do not feed the pigeons; they are dirty and they cause disease.
Don't encourage them. Ignore them and they might go away.

Please sir.

The stir, the hurry at dusk, scurrying home from the office,
bridging the gap, the rush for the train to whisk them away.
Then the quiet pause as the city dissolves in its evening drink
before the neon begins to make-up, outlining her face, her
pulse like a child's drawing: no shading, no subtlety, it's all
pulse and pace and Darlings and Dears and giggling pairs
wiggling past or striding to pick up their dates, ignoring the
faces as they ford the hunger.
And the neon screams
occasionally drown out the rat tat tat
of the approaching
train
sometimes sends a sliver of . . .
they shiver as they pause a moment to look at the lights as the
city thrusts herself forward etched in her . . .

Please sir

Look, if you strain your eyes, that hint of blue in the heart of the
city, that cold hush of blue creeping between the buildings, that's
the new multi-million pound . . .

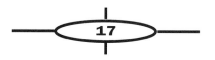

Lucky Lloyd that's what I say.

Excuse me please, can you . . .

Oh hurry hurry hurry past looking upoutdown away. Ignore
the shit in the streets. As long as you don't step on it you can
keep your shoes clean.

The debris collects in the corners.

Please sir.

They'll have to do something about it, really.

That one there, look there, Darling, that one is a girl. Is it really?

Well, who'd have thought it a girl living like this are you sure, not
that anybody could tell. I suppose we could ask her she must
know mustn't she if it is indeed a she. Or indeed if she is a he.

Perhaps for a quid she will show you her tits.

Don't be vulgar. Who'd want to see 'em old dugs anyway.

Probably crawling with fleas.

You know it doesn't just go away.

Please sir, the price of a cup of coffee.

There's ten pence for a tea.

What decade's this geezer living in, haven't seen tea for ten p.

in an age.

A meal?

I know about you. A liquid lunch, a strongbow supper. You
people, do you think that we don't know? Understand? Give you a
pound it'll shoot through, liquid, piss up a rope. Waste of time
really, isn't it? Took me three minutes to earn this pound. You'd
piss it away in that many seconds.

Can't you find somewhere less . . . public to sleep? You can't be

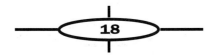

terribly comfortable there. All the noise. And these people
passing your . . . bed. I don't know how you manage a wink.

There's one. Is that lump one of them in the corner. No it's too
still; just rubbish I think.
Kick it and see if it moves.
Perhaps it's a body asleep, no it's just a bundle of rags.

Perhaps it will blow off into the river, the rubbish.

If a strong enough wind were to come up tonight, to blow out
the neon, the words sliding across the facade of the theatre,
the colours shimmying up the side of the gallery, the teasing
come-on of the city . . . Perhaps such a wind is brewing already,
the sort of wind which would clear it all away.

Already the debris drifts off the bridge into the river, bobbing a
moment before the current sweeps it off or the tangle of
underwater weeds traps it, grabs it, pulling it under . . .
But it won't disappear.
It returns a few miles or a few winters away in the weeds by
the banks.
Nothing ever disappears for ever.

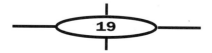

ON BLUE PETER

JOHN HEGLEY

If more homeless people had tellies
Would they show you how best to make
 homes out of cardboard?
Maybe they should anyway
For kids in houses now
Who might appreciate the knowhow later.

SHORT STOREY

JOHN HEGLEY

Life in a box
isn't necessarily a ball
but one of the advantages of cardboard houses
is that banging your head against the wall
is painless.

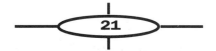

**ELL THE TRUTH
DAD PISSED ME
OFF AND MAM**
could never cope. I'm on my own
and watching out for winter now. Cold wet fart
roused me this morning in a travel agent's door.

A binbag mac keeps out the rain
and polystyrene warms your soles;
Guardian and *Times* lag best; you keep *The Sun*
to twist a jam rag for your bum.

Remember remember the fifth of November —
coat off a guy or maybe kecks; and two left shoes
knocked off from outside Timpson's
are better than no shoes at all.

Empty paint cans burn and after you can boil
one for a brew. Back of Tesco's
for dumped unlabelled tins — dog and cat
but now and then you hit on pilchards, mince.

Down the cemetery — diggers' cabin's good,
stove still warm, enough tobacco shreds
around the floor to make a roll — out of
the wind, the way.

Cold morning piss-smells and white
tiles where you wash, where you never take
off coats. Look out for Number One's the game . . .
there's always someone needier.

NOVEMBER ON THE STREETS

MATT SIMPSON

SAFE PLACES
MARK ILLIS

How does a ticket collector spend his time when he's not collecting tickets? On a fast train, when he hasn't got too much to do, where is he? What is he up to? On a slow train they're busy, they come out after every station, up and down, trying to register faces, checking your ticket and your railcard and whether you've got your feet up on the seat opposite, and whether you're taking up too much space with your luggage, and whether you're slashing the cushions. When they see someone like me it's like they've turned into border guards and they're going to shine a torch into my face and want to know what's in my bag and what's the purpose of my journey. Usually they don't see me.

I got a fast train, like a careful commuter, and he never came out much. God knows how he was passing the time, so it was just a matter of knowing where to be and when to be there to stay out of his way. You get used to avoiding people, you get, after a while, a knack for it. Half the idea of being on the train was to avoid someone. It had been a bad week in which getting chucked out of a hostel was only the beginning. Half the idea was to avoid someone, half the idea was to see someone. For once I had a purpose. This felt fine. Four seats to myself, a nice normal family opposite, and two businessmen behind. This was all right.

When I wasn't jumping out of my seat at the sight of a blue uniform I was quite relaxed. I expected to be nervous, but I wasn't. I just didn't think about where I was going, I just took it easy, not thinking about anything much, staring out of the window, taking my time, taking my time, watching the hundred miles an hour towns and fields and roads and rivers, letting them hypnotise me, thinking I should take the train more often, thinking I could spend a lot of time on trains, as long as I avoided babies and Walkmans and ticket collectors.

Of course, there was a bit of space around me. Usual thing. A few glances thrown my way, by the nice family on the other side, or the people swaying down the aisle with their little bags of sandwiches. It's not so much as if they're curious, because what is there to see? It's more as if they're checking the distance between us, checking I'm not too close, checking I'm not getting any closer. You find yourself a lot of the time on the fringe of things. On the fringe of people's attention, at the corners of their eyes, at the edge of the pavement. You're the poignant detail in someone's picture of St Martin's. It gives you a different angle, encourages you to look at everything sideways. Words for instance. Take these: Social Security. What's that about? It sounds like it should be something about being secure in society, but it can't be that. Some mistake there you'd have to say. Do you know what it really reminds me of? Security guards, bouncers maybe, policemen, ticket collectors, all of them working for some exclusive club that you're not a member of.

So I leant my head against the window, and let the glances brush over me like light, curious fingers. It's not a problem. I'm good at being on my own, I'm an expert. The only problem was thinking about those sandwiches.

The closer I got, of course, the more I remembered to be nervous. The day before, when I was feeling fairly low about everything, it had seemed like a flash of genius. First the hostel, that was Monday, then three kids with knives had taken off me the few quid I'd made, that was Tuesday, and then I had trouble with some man who I really didn't like being near me. 'You look like you could use a meal,' he says. Not that badly, I'm thinking. So when it came to me, I thought I was brilliant, but the closer I got the less it seemed like a good idea. Fewer thoughts about trains and ticket collectors, more about my destination. The idea had been to escape, as far as there was any idea at all. I hadn't thought it through.

By the time I got there I didn't know what to do, I was off the train before it had even stopped, running a few paces down the platform, but I was probably last out of the station, dragging my feet. It was all the wrong way round, but it was now that I felt like I was trespassing. Now that I was in familiar surroundings, I felt completely out of place. I was scared shitless that I'd see someone I knew. Still, I kept moving in the right direction. I dawdled, and stopped to look in shop windows, and took an indirect route, but I was approaching all the time, not actually circling but zig-zagging, like I was creeping up on some beast, on some wild animal.

I must have looked shady, but no one stopped me, no one looked twice. I was nearly there, in spite of myself, I was actually at the end of the road, just beginning to ask myself outright for the first time — what the fuck am I doing here? — when I saw it. I stopped. I stopped and stared for a while and sort of looked up and down the road. Sometimes you need to see other people's reactions before you know what your own should be. No one else around. What was I supposed to make of this? By this time I'd thought of a hundred possibilities, but this was unexpected. I got a bit closer, until I could see the house. Looked it up and down. No clues there. The doors shut and the curtains drawn. As far as I could tell, what it looked like was, all the furniture had just been taken out of the house and left there, in the garden and on the street. I mean all the furniture, like the house had spewed it all out in some kind of allergic reaction.

Time for plan B then. I'd anticipated that nobody might be there, and I'd said to myself if that was the case I'd wait. I'd been thinking they might be at the shops or something, not halfway through moving house, but it made no real difference. I'd wait. I didn't really hesitate much at all. I just sat down on an armchair, like I owned it. It wasn't one from the sitting-room, it was one that used to be in my room, so I felt comfortable with it. My old desk was nearby, so everything was familiar. Admittedly the desk was upside-down and everything was in the front garden, but apart from that, apart from that everything was familiar. Three piece suite, magazine rack, coffee table, standard lamp, rug, picture, three-bar fire, television. It struck me as funny. It was the way they would go about being homeless. They'd lose the roof but they'd take everything else with them. All this stuff would be spaced around them in the doorway on the Strand, and they'd be doing their best to look casual, like they belonged there. I smiled at this, and sat down on this old armchair, sank into it, deep, and I felt fine, began to relax again. I reached up to the lamp and switched it on. I put my feet up on the table. I stared at the TV. I felt fine.

People passed, and slowed down and looked at me as they went. They were a bit less inhibited about it than usual, having a bit more excuse. I ignored them. I felt self-sufficient. My own company again. It suits me well, I've found I can do without other people. Certain individuals are all right, but strangers, and particularly groups, are something else. I like my own space. Unfortunately in this situation, in the situation that I'm in, you meet all sorts. You get someone who wants to take you home with him, or rob you, or some drunk bastard who wants to give you a kicking, or someone who's been chucked out of some home and he's talking to himself, or shouting at people, or acting like he knows you and you've been following him. This happened to me. It's tricky. What are you supposed to do? You can't persuade him that he's wrong, you can't say, 'I'm sorry you must be mistaken.' I tried to reason with him and he got so insistent he started to convince me. Maybe I have been following this man. Maybe I do want something from him? To talk to him? To make him understand who I am, where I'm from, and what has happened to me? You have to just walk away, it's the only safe thing to do.

'Young man.' I looked up, and recognised Mr Norris, a neighbour of about ten years. He was standing on the low garden wall, looking at me like I was a stain on the carpet or something. 'What precisely do you think you are doing?'

My hand moved across my mouth. 'Waiting.'

He was peering at me more closely. 'You're making yourself comfortable.'

'Van should be here any time.'

He nodded, but gazed at me for a few seconds more.

'My boys should be here any time,' I said, surprising myself. 'We'll clear this lot, don't worry.'

I had dropped my hand from my face now, and was staring straight back at him. Mr Norris made a sound in his throat, and then walked on.

I felt like running after him. I wanted to ask, How much has nearly a year in London changed me? Don't you recognise me? Aren't you curious? Weren't you ever curious about what happened to me? I wouldn't have

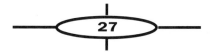

minded answers to these questions. I knew I'd never played an important part in his life, but I thought he might have wondered, idly, what had become of me. He would have heard half the arguments through the wall. He would have heard what the arguments developed into. It's stupid, but I like to play with this fantasy that people had sympathy for me, that they whispered behind closed doors about my step-father. On bad nights, when for one reason or another I couldn't sleep, I might even imagine people at home lying awake wondering about me, feeling sorry for me, even out looking for me. Probably he was just glad that the noise had stopped.

This was turning over in my mind, I might have been back on the train because I was dreaming really, when the next thing happened. It's a part of the situation that I'm in: I don't do very much, but now and then things happen to me. It's all right with me, you get happy to stay in one place after a while, and let things happen around you. I still hadn't even planned what I'd do when they came back, I was just sitting there, thinking about things fairly randomly, letting things happen.

A child ran into the garden.

He rushed in there like there was someone chasing him and then stopped suddenly, as if he'd been a bit bolder than he'd intended.

He said, 'What are you doing?'

This was the kind of interruption I didn't mind.

'I'm sitting here,' I said, 'watching the world turn around. What are you doing?'

He laughed. The situation seemed to please him and he jumped on to the sofa opposite my chair. He sat up to face me. 'Why?' he said, still chuckling, as if possibly all this furniture had been placed here, and I was sitting here, as part of some elaborate joke that I was soon going to reveal.

I shook my head, smiling, trying to tell him with a shrug of my shoulders that the joke was hidden from me as well, I wasn't going to explain anything. Why am I sitting here? Why has the house turned inside out? I don't know. I don't know. Don't ask me, because I don't know. I'd thought about things quite a lot, looked back at events, at the way things happened, asked myself how I got where I am, to the situation I am in. You don't get easy answers. You don't get to say, This is what happened, these acts of violence led to this, which in turn created a different set of circumstances, which is the world that I am living in. What happened is more complicated than that, because I do not know why it happened, whether it could have been prevented, and whether my reaction was correct. What happened is that words that should have one meaning turned out to have another. Family. Care. Benefit. None of these things mean what you think they mean. Or they mean more than one thing, they shift, in a different light they surprise you, turn around, turn inside out, turn on you.

I said to the child, 'I like sitting here. It's nice here, isn't it?' Because I was enjoying having his company, although where his parents were I didn't know, and whether they'd be glad he was out on his own talking to a stranger.

He seemed to be about to answer, and then looked past me, suddenly scared.

'Hey!'

I turned round. The look on Mr Norris's face would have scared anyone.

'I know you, don't think I didn't know you, you've caused your parents nothing but grief. How dare you come back here? How dare you come back here?' He was ranting. He had pushed through the garden gate, and he had the child, who was now crying, by the arm. He snapped at him, 'Come with me Timmy, you're going back to your mother.' And then at me, 'What have you been saying to him? What have you done to him? You better not be here when I come back, or I'll be dialling 999.'

As I say, I don't do very much, but things happen around me. Timmy was dragged off screaming, and Mr Norris was looking over his shoulder, still shouting at me, as he stamped off down the street, pleased with himself I'd guess. What was behind all that? What had they told him about me? It's not just words that you can't trust, it's not just words that turn on you.

I got up, not comfortable any more, not happy any longer to just sit there.

HOUSING ASSOCIATIONS FIND IT INCREASINGLY DIFFICULT TO ACCOMMODATE YOUNG PEOPLE, SINCE THEY ALREADY FIND IT HARD TO COPE WITH THE PRESSURE OF HOUSING HOMELESS FAMILIES, WHICH TAKE PRIORITY.

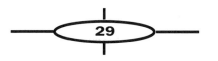

I got out of my old, deep armchair and went up to the front door and tried it, locked of course, so went round to the side, to the kitchen window I used to use. Sure enough it was open and I could stand on the sill and reach in, to the bigger window, and open that, and climb through, jumping down to the floor in my muddy shoes that Mum would have had a fit about. I had just wanted to see her. I could not explain why. The truth is I had no plans, because I am not in a position to make plans. I didn't intend any violence, originally I didn't even intend to talk to them. We have nothing to say to each other, there are no words for us. I hoped to catch sight of them, to see them moving about the business of an ordinary day. I had a feeling that I might learn something about them in that way. I don't know what I hoped to learn. I don't know what to think about them. A clue towards that would have been enough.

I moved around the house. It was more than empty, it was stripped. Furniture, curtains, carpet, appliances, even one or two cupboards which had been attached to the wall. There was nothing here to evoke a memory or create a response, nothing to provoke a sense of atmosphere. I trailed my hand along bare walls, and stood in doorways, trying to picture furnished and peopled rooms. Arguments, confrontations, some things were well-known from dreams as well as memories, but I could not achieve anything larger, anything suggestive of a broader period, of part of a life, of a childhood. No story adheres to me. I do not live in the world of actions and relationships, my horizons have been narrowed. I concentrate on surviving. I live in the corner of people's eyes, in darting glances. What I would like is not very much. A safe place, to recover myself, to think about a new story for myself, to learn how to begin. Wherever ticket collectors go on trains, that would be a safe place. At the moment it is impossible to begin. Too much is vivid. I felt it again moving around the house, after Mr Norris's abuse, rediscovering pain that I thought had faded, my hand moving slowly over my body, as if over a map, tracing landmarks. Perhaps it's not so difficult to find a simple chain of events: this happened (my hand was on my arm); and then this (over my ribs); and then this, and this. Grief, he had said, I had caused my parents grief. That is a phase I have largely passed through. After grief comes something else. Anger. There is

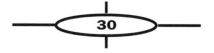

an anger in my heart that I can't calculate. It is immense.

When the van eventually arrived, it woke me from a doze. Two men in overalls were picking up the sofa opposite me and carrying it out of the garden. Another came in and picked up the light and the heater.

'Who are you then?'

'I'm the son.'

He looked at me sceptically. 'You coming with us then?'

This was an interesting idea. To travel in the van, and to be carried out, on my armchair, like part of the furniture, to be placed in the sitting-room or a bedroom, occupying my space.

I thought about it for a few seconds, and then became aware of the man staring at me. 'No,' I said, 'I'll follow.'

The three men came and went, removing every item, fitting everything with surprising ease into the cavernous van, until eventually I had to get up, abandoning my armchair, so they could remove that too. They moved off sluggishly at first, but accelerated before turning out of sight, leaving me to think about trains, and ticket collectors, and whether I might safely postpone the return journey, to spend a night in the empty, unfamiliar house behind me.

YOU LEAVE IN THE MORNING

With everything you own
In a little black case
Alone on a platform
The wind and the rain
On a sad and lonely face

Mother will never understand
Why you had to leave
For the love that you need
Will never be found at home
And the answer you seek
Will never be found at home

Pushed around and kicked around
Always a lonely boy
You were the one
That they'd talk about around town
As they put you down
And as hard as they would try
They'd hurt to make you cry
But you'd never cry to them
Just to your soul
No you'd never cry to them
Just to your soul

PUSHED AROUND AND KICKED AROUND

SMALLTOWN BOY

JIMMY SOMERVILLE/

LARRY STEINBACHEK/

STEVE BRONSKI/

**WE THOUGHT OF
ASHFIELD AND
IMAGINED TREES;**
wood smoke, horses and the ricochet of hooves,
a meltwater stream
like milk from the moors,

beehives, bird life, allotments, a breeze.
Like bloodhounds now we track the moment of the truth,
by which I mean
the way we choose

to say which quaver tipped the song into a scream,
to pinpoint how the pinprick widened to a bruise
for you, for me.
I'll list the clues:

the so-called ash, the field, the so-called streets
at sixes, sevens, German shepherds in their schools
of threes
and twos,

IT IS NOW IMPOSSIBLE TO GET A COUNCIL FLAT THROUGH THE WAITING LIST IN MANY PARTS OF THE COUNTRY BECAUSE OF REDUCTIONS IN COUNCIL HOUSING STOCK.

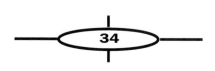

for peace of mind this baseball bat, for sleep
these tablets and a certain ratio of booze
will count for sheep
and see us through.

We idle now on waiting lists, and dream
of runways, level crossings, traffic queues;
waiting to come clean,
to break the news

of how we live, of what we have seen,
of how it leaves us, and what that proves.
A light goes green,
but nobody moves.

NOTICE
TO QUIT

SIMON ARMITAGE

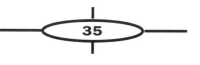

OUT LOUD
A Nobody's Proclamation
SAM NORTH

I'm fucked.
It's money. Money.
Give me.
I'm not deserving, I don't earn.

Home is where your heart
— my heart?
Only asking.

Understand
I'm not begging, crucial that, I'm not doing
this to get pity.

More pity, please.

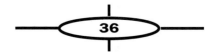

Often I daydream about violence and about
what will become good or bad when now is
past

(I can imagine myself heroic).

The keys to a place, a fringe of cool metal
and vacant possession

takes money, willpower
takes luck that won't come
takes money and will and luck
and good, and solid, and reliable behaviour.

But mostly money.

An inheritance, a job or a gift.
A magic penny in my pocket that is replaced
the instant I withdraw it. I could buy an
Escort Turbo afterwards — a penny at a time,
it would take days.

Dreams of finding a suitcase full of cash
won't do.

You have to ignore the look of someone,
d'you know that. So get used to the idea
now
and get beyond it
and grow good and wise before your time.

Your wife or husband will be ugly one day,
sick, unhappy
— you too.

So don't mind me swearing when you don't.

Or I might have the self-control necessary
to do it properly: being super, super-nice
whatever.

You will prefer it if
I dance for you, play or juggle.

It's not me
nor anything I want to do. I'm too
meaningful for that really, apart from as an
act.

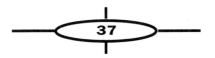

These words, I'll take all of them for
myself. I need some form of plenty.

God visit me.

God
— your mysterious ways hurt like hell.

Fuck off with your help

(just a cry for help, that is).

Because we all have our terrible stories.
Want to know mine? I've beaten it out, I
have it ready here.

Perhaps it's better if you hear some nice
ones first, like the one about the old derro
who wrote a book and begged enough money to
pay to print it himself; now he stands and
flogs it for a nifty profit.

Or the guy who got handed on a plate vacant
possession of a two-bed, plus housing
benefit to pay for it and found himself so
bored and so out of place so
he went back to The Strand.

But there are terrible stories — you've
heard them all before. They're not stories.

And stupidness as thick as glue holding a
whole load of us down here below you lot.

Marylai North

A SNAPSHOT:
24 HOURS ON THE STREETS OF BRISTOL
Jack O'Sullivan reports on a night spent with the Clan

A man in a leather jacket squares up to the eighteen-year-old beggar, their faces inches apart. 'I've warned you before and the message seems to be sinking in very slowly,' he shouts. 'If I catch you around here again, you're nicked.'

This is the Pit, a sunken roundabout where Bristol's homeless people — including Paul, Jock, Jim, Sharon, Sara and Wayne, of the Clan — gather together. Paul has made the mistake of chanting: 'Can you spare a bit of change, please' as two plain clothed CID officers pass by.

'That one has already arrested me seven times,' Paul (an alias) explains later. 'I'm going to have to leave Bristol.' He has been there for six months and jailed overnight nine times, under the increasingly used 1824 Vagrancy Act.

It has been a miserable day. Begging is poor, raising only half the £20 daily average that the Clan members generally share out. Income Support of £31.50 approximately, has been spent. Good earners, such as going on identity parades for a fiver, have dried up. The previous evening, Bristol's night shelter was closed despite gales. Tonight the Clan walk in heavy rain to a multi-storey carpark.

On the ninth floor, blankets are spread over concrete. The group all wrap up over their wet clothes and share two bottles of cider. They sleep in soaked training shoes rather than risk losing them to a passing thief. Strip-lighting blazes all night. At 11.30pm a policeman arrives, but tonight lets them stay put, saying he won't move them unless there are complaints.

Everyone is relieved. 'That's the first time they haven't made us leave,' says Jock.

Jock, a former paratrooper, at 33 is the grand old man of the Clan. He's been homeless for four years since leaving the army after six tours of duty in Northern Ireland.

No one sleeps properly because of the cold. At eight in the morning, when the first motorist steps over the makeshift bedding and bodies to get to the lift, everyone is awake. It is Sharon's 17th birthday.

The Clan heads for tea at McDonald's carrying their blankets in bin liners. Then it's on to the day centre, run by Bristol Cyrenians, which opens at 9.30am. Here there's three and a half hours of domesticity: hot showers, clean clothes, tea on

tap, fried egg on toast and vegetable pie for lunch.

Then, at 1pm, it's back on to the streets to fill the hours until the night shelter opens after nine. It's still raining.

We walk endlessly, chatting about unsteady, needy lives. Paul says that he ran away from home at 12, after being beaten by his stepfather. At 16, after three year's working in a fair, then one in care, he got a flat, thanks to his father paying a deposit, and a job pipelaying. By 17, he had an £8,000 car. Then the job fell through: 'I sold the car for five and a half grand, but on the way home I went past a casino and blew the lot. I'm addicted to gambling.' Paul already has a three-year-old child.

Sara, 20, was 'kicked' out of home two years ago. At the day centre's creative writing class, her prose reveals the six overdoses she has taken in the last year.

With 'no fixed abode' none can find jobs. Wayne, 20, from Belfast explains: 'When Jim and I came to Bristol first we were so smart we still had creases in our shirts. But if you're NFA you get no work. You look scruffy and they are afraid of you. They think you could be anyone especially if you're Irish.

And we can't find a place to live. Landlords want deposits, which we don't have and the Social Security won't give us.'

The only alternatives are hostels which are either full or so primitive that the street seems attractive. The Clan describe a hostel offering tiny cubicles filled mainly by the old, the mentally ill, and alcoholics. There had been several fires there, and someone had committed suicide by diving down a spiral staircase.

The Clan walk on with much of the day still to kill. 'On New Year's day, we spent hours down there in that toilet, sheltering from the rain,' Jim says.

At 9.30pm the night shelter doors finally open on to a vast factory floor, sprinkled with old bedsteads, nowhere to change and only mobile toilets. Volunteers serve food.

But there is a tense atmosphere; drunken brawls break out every few minutes and the Clan members find themselves caught up.

At midnight, the police throw them out. They sigh with relief — there is at least peace outside — and it's a return to the relative sanctuary of another night in the freezing carpark.

And Paul says :

'We have to wait until maybe we get a home or a break. Maybe we'll meet someone who'll give us a start.'

(A full length version of the above piece was originally published in *The Independent*, and the publishers gratefully acknowledge their kind permission to reprint it in this collection.)

BLUES FOR VINCENT

GEOFF DYER

Whoever has no home now will never have one
Whoever is alone now will be alone forever.

RILKE

It must be four years ago that I first saw Zadkine's sculpture of Vincent and Theo Van Gogh — not even the actual statue, just a maquette — in one of the museums in Amsterdam. Carved in angular-cubist style, the sculpture is of two men sitting, one with his arm around the other's shoulders. I think their heads are touching but I could easily be wrong (works of art that affect you deeply are seldom quite as you remember them). Unusually for a piece so thoroughly committed to the language of cubism, the sculpture works on us very simply, directly addressing the humanity of its subjects where normally the cubist effect distorts and dislocates. Rarely has the hardness of stone been coaxed into such softness.

Zadkine wanted his sculpture to express the relationship of dependency and trust that existed between Vincent and his brother. By depicting an actual moment — as opposed to embodying the idea of fraternity in an abstract form — he reminds us that certain gestures, however light, contain the emotional weight of a lifetime. Very specifically, Zadkine's sculpture reveals all the tenderness of which men are capable of offering each other. (Everything about the sculpture would be different if it showed a similar relationship between a man and a woman.)

It is not immediately obvious which of Zadkine's figures is Vincent and which is Theo. Like all who relieve the suffering of others, Theo — in a process which is the exact opposite of a blood transfusion — has taken some of Vincent's pain into himself. Soon, however, it becomes obvious that while the sky weighs heavily on both figures, one, Vincent, feels the gravity as a force so terrible it can drag men beneath the earth. From this moment on, you are held by the pathos and beauty of what Zadkine depicts: despair that is inconsolable, comfort that is endless. One figure says: *I can never feel better*, the other: *I will hold you until you are better*.

Looking at the sculpture, you internalise the dialectic of the piece: I will never feel pain like Vincent's . . . but I will never encounter tenderness like Theo's. Perhaps it is only possible to sense the scale of Vincent's isolation if, looking at Theo, you realise that never will you be able to offer anyone even a fraction of his tenderness.

A few hundred yards from where I am now living, between Avenues A and B in what used to be known as Alphabet City, is Tompkins Square, a park taken over almost completely by a few hundred of New York's thousands of homeless. 2nd Street, just off Avenue A, is one of the main crack and heroin dealing blocks in lower Manhattan. This evening someone was grabbing his head and hurling himself at a storefront, falling to the floor screaming, lying still for a few seconds and then, exhausted but still in the grip of this frenzy, picking himself up and doing it again. An hour later he was unconscious on the sidewalk.

Each morning people are sprawled in the streets, so deeply comatose that even the indifferent kicks of cops fail to rouse them. Throughout the day the destitute and the addicted, the insane and the desperate, sit in pairs in doorways and on steps, heads bowed, hearing each other out or reaching out an arm while the other groans and shivers.

I see your face everywhere, wandering through it like rain and the drifting steam of streets. I wake at four in the morning and think of you doing ordinary things: washing, hunting for your glasses that you can never find or picking up shopping in a supermarket, the people at the check-out seeing you.

Before I unlock the mailbox I can tell if there is a letter from you. I long

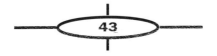

for your letters and dread the announcements and decisions they might
contain, spend whole days waiting for you to call.

I pick up the phone on the second ring, hear an American voice say,

'Hi, how ya doin'?'

'Fine.'

'What's happenin'?'

'Who is this?'

'I'm just somebody callin' up.'

'What about?'

'I'm just a guy hangin' out. So how ya doin'?'

'What?'

'Ah, I'm feelin' kind of low.'

'So I don't know you?'

'No.'

'I can't talk to you.'

'No . . .?'

As if he had *eternity* on his hands.

At eight — one in the morning English time — I call you, the familiar
English tones becoming bleak after six rings. In case you are just coming
through the door I let it ring another ten times, hoping that when you get
back you will be able to tell I have called, furniture and walls preserving a
message there was no answering machine to receive: I miss you, I want
you, I love you. Then I just let it ring, the phone pressed to my head like a
pistol.

The closing session of David Murray's week-long stint at a club in
Greenwich Village: halfway through the set he announces 'Ballad for the
Black Man'.

'Ballad for the nigger,' says a friend in the audience.

'Yeah, man, ballad for the nigger.'

Murray started off as an energy player but in recent years he's been
digging back into the tradition and now sounds like a whole history of the
tenor saxophone: in his playing you can hear Ayler, Coltrane, Rollins,

Webster . . .

In the same way 'Ballad for the Black Man' contained the cry of all the spirituals and sorrow songs, all the blues there have ever been. Murray's solo lasted for ten minutes, climaxing with notes so high they disappeared, as if a part of the song were not addressed to human ears at all. The blues is like that, not something you play but a way of calling out to the dead, to all the dead slaves of America.

The message of the blues is simple: as long as there are people on earth they will have need of this music. In a way, then, the blues is about its own survival. It's the shelter the black man has built, not only for himself but for anyone who needs it. Not just a shelter — a home. No suffering is so unendurable that it cannot find expression, no pain is so intense that it cannot be lessened — this is the promise at the heart of the blues. It cannot heal but it can hold us, can lay a hand around a brother's shoulder and say:

You will find a home, if not in her arms, then here, in these blues.

(For Fi.)

FOUR VOICES
ADÈLE GERAS

If that one gives me owt, I'll show my arse
in M and S's window.

> I don't know what   a disgrace
> I call it   the world's coming to
> some of these kids   look at the starving
> Africans   got a cheek   don't   know
> they're born   look at the Kurds
> I don't know   before the War
> not to mention poor dumb animals
> absolutely shocking   where
> do they all come from?

I can read her mind, see?
Like her thoughts were them balloons
you get sometimes, puffy pink and silver.

> Bye baby bunting
> Daddy's buggered off.
>
> Rock a bye baby
> only quietly.
> Walls are thin.
>
> Rub a dub dub
> forty people
> use this bath.

Hickory dickory dock
the mouse ran
behind the skirting-board
when I opened the door.

Baa baa black sheep
bloody typical of you
said my Mum.
No one else in this
family ever
got in trouble.

id know a house
if i saw one   once
i was in a home
im a snail now
with a sleeping bag
curled up on my back
finding spaces
out of the rain
one pound fifty ninell
buy a burger an chips but
the needle cant wait   what
did it feel like
to be really full

There's him outside Oxfam
with a dead cute dog
that just sits there
looking hungry.   My old cat
would never stand for it.
She'd walk off if she wanted.
She's the one I think of.

She's the one I miss.
She's not the one I'm leaving.
She never hurt me.

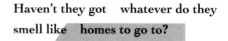

Haven't they got   whatever do they
smell like   homes to go to?

Bed and breakfast baby
better beware.
One little squeak
and they'll take you into care.

One little smack
on your pink little bum
then
in comes the doctor
in comes the nurse
and the magistrate lady
with the alligator purse
to take you away
from your poor old Mum.

So hush pretty baby
don't dare to cry.
I'll have towels like that
sheets like that
look at all the windows, lovey.
See that bed there? In't it smashing?
We'll have that one, thank you kindly
in the sweet bye and bye.

I'd write to my Mum if I had a stamp.
Dear Mum, I'd say, do you know that your house

your red brick terrace, all neat and prim,
(two up, two down,
privet hedges, garden path,
blue hydrangea by the door,
ding-dong silly
doorbell chimes,
microwave oven,
colour telly,
fluffy covers,
on the loo-seat, and all that)
is a monster's cave where the walls run blood?

see him over there
with his crimplene trousers
baggy an hanging
off his arse
you can just tell
hed do it with anything
must be good for a bob or two
o jesus i hope
i hope he is

Mum, do you know
about slimy fingers,
smelly breath, scaly skin?
Do you recognise him you married?
Him in the photo, slick and smug,
my Dad? I'm not stopping in his cave.

My squat's a bloody paradise
compared. I've got mates.
On a good day,
I have chips and a cuppa

and an apple off the barrows.
I can slice money
thin as bacon.
! can spot a decent fag-end
at a hundred paces.
I can smile nicely,
make rich mothers think:
that could be my daughter.
Then I'm laughing.

And in my day   no better than
they should   you kept yourself
to yourself   clean   some of this lot.
It's drugs   and it's
the system   and it's
the lack of discipline and it's
not enough love   and it's
what the world is coming to
I don't know   and it's

after the needle
im ok   im better
needle shines in my eyes
like a candle
i get a fiver if im lucky
an the back seat of a car
else its bum against the bricks
ta very much and heres
a bit of a change

needles need
thats why theyre called that
need feeding dont they

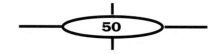

like fucking slot machines
like juke boxes
put a penny in an
up goes my skirt
an here comes the music
listen   o
i fancy a needle
something rotten   give us one

I blame the parents   and
I blame the teachers   and
I blame the Government   and
I blame television   and
I blame   I blame   and
why don't they all get jobs?
There.
That's the answer.   Fancy
no one thinking of that before!
When it comes right   at the end of
down to it   the day
I blame the Council.
They clear the litter, don't they?

Baby, I wish you
a front door
you can lock

A gas fire
and matches.

I wish you a fridge
with milk in it

A biscuit tin
full of Kitkats.

Pretty green cartons
full of orange juice

Enough money
at the checkout

so you never have
to put anything back.

Oh, my little darling
I wish you
your own room
with a Care Bear
on the pillow.

Sweet baby
please don't cry.

Sweet baby
please don't cry.

OUR NEIGHBOURS

just along the Cut, were old.
About 6.30, they'd drop in on us.
They'd see us by the door and come across.
Our manageress would shush them with her arms,
yell 'Out!' at them until they went away.
After the show, we'd hurry by their park.
(We weren't to give them cash — a waste. Their sort
would only spend our tenpences on drink:
Woodpecker, British sherry, wine and meths.)

The Old Vic's staff canteen was cheap and good —
the rather debby types who came to cook
were trained in cordon bleu. (One's husband used
to act as taster on each dish she made.
He brought his books in while he studied Law.)
Ushers and actors, dressers, Wardrobe, Props
all stoked up down there on their way to work —
pigeons in cream, rough patés, escalopes,
or mild, sweet curries in Jamaican style
with fresh banana and dried coconut,
steaks, salads, omelettes, rabbit stews and roasts,
mushrooms, glazed carrots, petits pois, courgettes,
cauliflower florets swimming in cheese sauce.
And then we used to get our rich desserts —
Black Forest cherry cake and rum gateaux,
pies, tarts, fruit salads, mousses, puddings, flans —
with pints of cream to pour on everything.

Each night the lavish leavings were chucked out
or taken home by Staff — the fridge was small —
together with odd opened pints of milk
and sandwiches the punters hadn't bought.
I got my taste for salmon from those days.

Our neighbours' luck improved. They got their share
when Peggy Ashcroft joined the company
(hidden to the waist in Beckett's *Happy Days*
or straitlaced in a doleful Ibsen play).
She'd hinted that the food might be more use
(better than Sally Army bread and soup)
to those who lived and slept across the way.
Her simple plan worked out — for days — until
a message filtered from the management . . .
The ethics of the thing were difficult —
Arts Council money was involved . . . The food
was subsidised for *us* not them.

OUR
NEIGHBOURS

FIONA PITT-KETHLEY

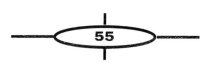

BOXED IN
JUNE OLDHAM

Lionel Paycock was, on his own admission, a man of high calibre whose public conscience went hand in glove with business success. He had inherited the principles of his great great grandfather who had flourished at the heyday of discriminating morality and he put these into practice, slightly tailored to the demands of the present time. For example, his belief in the sacredness of the family, his position as head in his own household, led to a degree of paternalism in his management of Paycock Containers: he had invested in a crèche for the babies of female operatives, though the reduction made from the mothers' wages brought in no return. His concern for the well-being of his own children was no less exemplary: he sent his daughters to a highly recommended secretarial college and, as financial consultant to the fund-raising committee at his son's school, gave advice on the acquisition of a third cricket pitch and a car park for the exclusive use of the Sixth.

Nor did his interest stop at the young and needy; as single shareholder of Paycock Properties, he built retirement bungalows for the widows of barristers which guaranteed their security, comfort and appropriate care. His own choice of home — the prerequisite for a stable family — was prompted by similar tenets, enhanced by his English nostalgia for the rustic and a somewhat subjective interpretation of Green. Originally a stone cottage picked up for a song, it had been sympathetically modernised and extended under his supervision into an olde worlde detached of immense character and charm, delighting in panoramic vistas to the front elevation and possessing four acres of mature woodland to the rear. At first, these had been somewhat marred by the seasonal encampment of travellers and

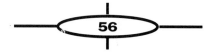

gypsies, but their antique rights, judged by his fellow borough councillors as an anachronism in a progressive society, had been annulled. A number of dogs, strategically positioned, had discouraged objection and, nothing if not fair, Lionel had proposed an alternative site adjacent to the corporation tip. To account for this prodigal altruism, he would say, 'I blush to confess it but, like my great great grandfather, I am philanthropic to a fault.'

This notorious characteristic was particularly evident early one winter when the meeting of borough councillors came to the last item on the agenda. 'Growth of rubbish on our streets and disposal of,' the Chairman intoned. 'You will remember, gentlemen, lady, that Refuse was instructed to deal with this. However, they report that the men returned, mission unaccomplished. The drivers of the bulldozers refused to go in. They claimed that their orders had not included the contents of these cardboard receptacles and they were worried about third party insurance.'

There followed a chorus of exclamations and comment:

'. . . really the limit . . . unions . . . not paid to question our. . .'

'. . . cannot understand the mentality . . . warm bed man, myself . . .'

'. . . poll tax evaders? Any mileage in the courts? . . .'

' . . . off the streets . . . preferably behind bars . . . honest citizens have the right to expect . . .'

'. . . tremendous co-operation . . . every garden a picture by next spring . . . Britain in Bloom . . . may prejudice our chances.'

One, noting the bewilderment of the woman, a newcomer to the Council, explained why her suggestion was impractical. 'Most of them sold off, I'm afraid. Council house tenants were most eager to optimize the opportunity. In spearheading the policy, we declared an interest in egality: creed, social orientation, even political colour, do not necessarily disqualify an Englishman from owning his own house.'

Another, overhearing this, added the rider: 'Also we had it on good authority that the waiting list was attracting the wrong sort. Young girls were getting themselves . . . in order to qualify for a place. As landlord for such tenants, we might have been thought guilty of encouraging immoral behaviour.'

The woman's enquiry concerning the hostel at Fenny Bottom drew similar

answers. It was soon to be demolished because the site was ear-marked for redevelopment. Once drains had been put in, there was to be a shopping complex plus everything from car washes to banks. Paycock Properties had it in hand.

A call to move progress, pronounced by a man impatient with unprofitable trifles, reminded the Chairman of his duty. From their comments it was clear that they spoke with one voice (giving an abbreviated glance at the woman). The scruples of Refuse must be eradicated forthwith — perhaps a threat of privatisation? — because, in view of the Council's campaign against litter, this household waste must no longer foul the streets. It must be redeployed.

His analysis was complimented by nods and 'hear, hear,' and all eyes turned to Lionel. When it came to redeployment, from an embarrassing trio of Boat People to a ragbag of gypsies, Lionel was their man. He smiled. He was ready.

'I see this problem as one of containment,' he began, then added, anticipating the wits: 'No doubt that is inevitable in my position as managing director of Paycock Containers plc. However, at this present moment in time I am thinking more along the lines of the other, the bricks and mortar, business in which I dabble a little.' He paused for the laughs. 'And it is apparent to me that here we have ribbon development when what is needed is something more compact. Whilst high-rise structures would have much to recommend them, they are impractical for the material to hand. So I am in favour of the good old-fashioned village green arrangement. It would receive the support of minor environmentalists, those of our constituents with Green Party leanings, and we can provide the space where it can grow naturally. Indeed, where it can enjoy *organic* growth! I propose that the police put up cones along the streets affected and divert obstructions to the stretch of derelict land behind Gasholder Road.'

Except for the new woman councillor who was as yet unversed in the complications of cleansing management, the meeting received his proposal with flattering enthusiasm. Before it was passed, however, one amendment was made. Since the ground was borough property, it represented capital which could realize interest. Therefore a rent for each plot was fixed and it was based on the nightly charge of the hostel before it was closed. Proposal and amendment were passed with but one dissenting vote.

It is always a pleasure to be pointed to a new source of income and though this was not directly Lionel's own, it held a promise of future spoil. When this land was put up for sale, its value would have appreciated because of the rents, therefore the gain to Paycock Properties, acting for the vendor, would proportionally increase. But private profit did not close Lionel's mind to public service; he was fond of assuring his constituents that, like his great great grandfather, he would direct his attention, when the need arose, to the common weal. He did so that evening with the following announcement: 'I have decided to make a personal contribution. In order to avoid an unsightly mess of units detrimental to the town's image, Paycock Containers will offer a free sample with every rented plot.'

The applause was still ringing in his ears the next morning when he went to his factory to order the delivery, and his gratification was heightened as he stood at the entrance and viewed his shop floor. Men at machines were stamping out cardboard; others operated laser knives; women, their patience and nimble fingers exactly suited to the fiddly task, were making up. There was nothing on the face of this earth, he would claim proudly, for which his work-force could not produce a container, and his products ranged from pill-boxes to an individual portaloo. This versatility owed much to the example of his grandfather who had once executed the ideal order: it combined craftsmanship, public hygiene, an OBE and stacks of cash. Its nature was never disclosed; Lionel sensed that, even in the less squeamish society of today, it might deter clients of Paycock Containers, and at the time, half a century ago, it was judged that the news of the County's preparation for enemy bombing, which took the form of a million papier mâché coffins, might not be good for morale. But placing, as it did, the business on a permanent foundation, that order held a special place in Lionel's heart; it inspired a pleasing sentiment and had a remarkable influence upon his artistic sensibilities. For, however original, neat, effective, were the boxes turned out by his factory, none provided him with

THE PRIVATE RENTED SECTOR PROVIDES ONLY 7% OF THE TOTAL HOUSING STOCK. TO SECURE PRIVATE RENTED ACCOMMODATION, A DEPOSIT IS NEARLY ALWAYS REQUIRED — TOO HIGH FOR MOST YOUNG PEOPLE TO AFFORD.

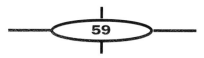

complete aesthetic satisfaction. He always hankered after the coffin shape.

Moved by this vision, he was disposed to stop when one of his female operatives approached him, and he listened with reasonable patience to her appeal: it was for his advice on how she should contact a missing member of her family.

'I think you are worrying unnecessarily, Mrs . . . Mrs . . . er . . .' he answered, graciously omitting to remind her that any submission to the Managing Director should be made through the prescribed channels. 'You should be proud that your daughter is set on trying her wings. Admirable. Quite admirable. Too many of today's young want life easy; they lack backbone and there is no military service to straighten them out. But your daughter, I'm glad to say, does not fall into that category and when you moved your ailing parents into your house and gave them her bed, she had a proper excuse. You have an adventurous young woman on your hands, Mrs . . . Mrs . . . er . . . She is fit — will soon grow out of that asthma, because, believe me, there is nothing like the open air life,' he told her, ignoring a dismal night which as a wolf cub he had spent in a tent. 'It is to her credit that she begins afresh without employment or capital. Clearly she belongs to that great English tradition of the self-made, as I do myself, or,' he added, to make his point intelligible, 'Dick Whittington.'

'He had a cat,' the woman murmured, demonstrating the usual female interest in trivia, but she admitted that mothers were frequently over-protective. The trouble was, she had always imagined her daughter in a nice comfortable little house of her own, when she was grown up.

Lionel expressed the hope that, if that day came, she would call upon the expertise of Paycock Properties. In deference to fashion, he might occasionally give time to counselling, but it replenished no coffers.

At last in his office, Lionel summoned his works manager and issued instructions: cartons must be withdrawn and sent to Dispatch. But the man, bewildered by this lapse into charity, needed guide-lines. 'You'll be meaning seconds?' he asked.

The answer seemed obvious but there was the firm's reputation to consider. Lionel decided he could not risk delivery of faulty or imperfect goods.

The works manager pursed his lips. However, it was not for him to object. 'And what about size?' he demanded. 'Do you want them to be all the same, or mixed: singles, doubles, and Kings? And we've a few Emperors left in store.'

Lionel judged that the last two might encourage undesirable practices but it would be reasonable to include a few of the doubles to be distributed to the Darbys and Joans. We must not forget that the family is the bedrock of our society.

Alarmed, the other regarded his employer and wondered whether he had missed earlier signs. 'Are they to go flat or made up?'

After some thought, Lionel chose flat. It was the era of DIY — in his opinion industry's greatest triumph of the century, passing the cost of assembly on to the customer without reducing the price — and learning how to fold and secure their own cartons would provide employment for idle hands.

His suspicions lulled slightly, the works manager asked whether he should select plastic-lined ones that kept out the wet.

'What do you think I am, some bloody bishop?' his employer demanded. 'They'll have the regular, and like it.'

'So we've no need to worry,' the works manager later concluded his account to his wife. 'The mortgage is still safe because though he may be

going a bit eccentric, he's not entirely out of his box.'

Unknown to him, however, the works manager's questions had had a profound effect. Concerned with carton quality and user-friendly features, they had taken root in Lionel's imagination. This was a thin, grudging soil and generally left fallow but, when dressed with the correct manure, capable of bearing fat fruit. Before the day was over, despite the distraction of a liquid lunch and nine unsteady holes of golf, Lionel had the skeleton of a new venture worked out.

It amounted to a vision.

Indeed, standing in his sympathetically modernised cottage of character and charm, looking out at the panoramic vistas to the front elevation, he could see it come to pass. His eyes misted with emotion, he beheld across the length and breadth of the land, serried ranks of container homes. Not pre-fabs, old railway coaches, dilapidated caravans, collapsing shacks — all those old-fashioned gimcracks favoured by recluses, drop-outs, Bolsheviks and artists — but solid, well cut and assembled packs, each one having individual fittings at the purchaser's choice. Not since those intoxicating days of the great Papier Mâché Order had a member of the Paycock dynasty laid his finger so confidently on the pulse of his customers; and in conformity with the gilded ethics of his inheritance, Lionel responded to market demands.

Delighted that his vision could embrace his two main businesses, he set up a new company, Paycock Container Properties. He experimented with new brands of cardboard; he started a subsidiary to manufacture his own; he initiated designs; he hired a stand at a national exhibition; he displayed show-packs in city squares. The interest and excitement his products caused was phenomenal. Before a single unit had been sold, he had a waiting list that would absorb the production of a whole year.

Yet, in the midst of success, a drawback was encountered. Profit demands energetic commitment and occasionally sacrifices have to be made. This was not wholly appreciated by his wife and family. When he asked his daughters to help with the presentation of the show-packs by made. This was not wholly appreciated by his wife and family. When he

asked his daughters to help with the presentation of the show-packs by demonstrating their comfort and fit, they refused. When he requested his son to investigate the current models available to users, he declined on the grounds that he would meet too many mates from his old school. Worse than these bewildering rebuffs was his wife's subversive reaction to his report of the customer waiting-list: she began to cook great vats of soup. For a man who had always governed his household benevolently and fairly, their disloyalty was painful. But, confident that when sales began his dependants would see the light, he paid no attention to his daughters' departure (destination unknown) or to the news of his son's marriage (decidedly unsuitable) or to his wife's absence throughout the night hours. He had more important matters to absorb him. Paycock Container Homes were in production; the packs were dropping off the conveyor belt; the delivery vans were lined up. There remained only one detail to clarify.

As he took his seat in the Council chamber one evening in mid-winter, he began, 'First let me say how gratified I am to have your interest in my new product.'

'My dear fellow, it was your proposal that removed the nuisance off our streets, so if you know of any assistance we can offer, just fire away,' the Chairman answered.

Another added, 'And you tidied up the disposal area by handing out free receptacles.'

Lionel smiled. 'Well, I'm afraid I could not leave it at that. As you know, I am the, often unhappy, possessor of a public conscience and so I could not entirely ignore the recipients of those first containers. It seemed to me that they should be encouraged to recognize their social responsibilities and that, to my way of thinking, is not to be satisfied with accommodation given free gratis but to invest in their own. Hence this brochure. If you glance through, you will note that, in line with present trends, all units are designed to reflect individual taste. My research team reports that the potential customers are more varied than you would predict, old winoes are now in the minority, but their needs have been catered for in the shanty model, 105, not dissimilar to 104, the basic economy pack. The rest conform to national standards and have been carefully planned to offer a wide range of choice and price. The bijou residence with deceptively spacious proportions is available to the first-time buyer, whereas the retirement flats will attract the older range. The ranch-style will delight those who remember the empire, as also will the grass hut. The mews and marina versions, though compact, share that unique smartness, whereas the back-to-back terrace module re-creates all the warmth and fellowship of the industrial street. Renovated as the Tudor residence, with a veneer of lath and plaster, this naturally becomes one of our most luxurious buys. Notice, too, its special feature, not repeated elsewhere: a cat door. This idea was suggested to me by one of my female operatives and I included it since we had to retire her husband after an accident and this seemed the most satisfactory way of giving compensation.

'Not only, may I add, are these packs purpose-designed, but they are made to last. They have, finally, a unique feature of which I am very proud. They can be recycled. Or, perhaps, it would be more exact to say, adjusted. Should any customer be unable to continue the weekly payment at the original level, all we have to do is lift off the transfers and replace them with the appropriate set. In the twinkling of an eye, we can transform a Dales millstone grit frontage to contiboard and wire mesh!

'Now you will recognize that these units, their design, production and marketing, represent no small investment,' he continued, but was interrupted by cries of congratulation. The response was not unanimous, however. When it had quietened, the woman councillor asked, 'May I enquire whether your public conscience extends to youngsters? I imagine that your research team uncovered them?'

'Indeed it has,' Lionel answered, smiling, 'and you will find their model illustrated at the back of the brochure. It is called the Paycock Starter Home. The idea was given to me by one of my female operatives, the very same who suggested the cat door, Mrs . . . Mrs . . . er . . . '

'Sparrow,' the woman councillor supplied, tight- lipped. 'She and I are in touch.'

'. . . and frankly, I predict that it will be one of our most popular lines, not only because it is cheaper to produce in large quantities, but because less material is required. Customers for our Starter Homes are lighter, they

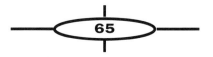

favour a modest diet, and their average dimensions are less. Indeed, my research team reports that, even during these winter months, there has been a notable reduction in size. This is, happily, in accordance with our thinking. Starter Homes are easy to manage, cosy, and what is more important, compact. These youngsters do not collect belongings and thus do not require the same facilities as the more settled age groups. They prefer to improvise, so we have included no fittings except the ventilating perforated disk with finger-tip control. They are installed, pre-sale, with each pack. I have to admit to you that I have absolutely no doubt that these Starter Homes, the Paycock Container Properties module 106, will be the thing of the future and I have donated, not entirely for publicity reasons, one of these Starter Homes to each of my daughters.'

This announcement was received with ecstatic applause, though serious cautions were voiced against such philanthropy. It could be taken too far, a danger which, it was agreed, should not be risked. Heads round the table nodded. Supplied with this cue, the Chairman recalled a government scheme to subsidise first home building provided it was carried out by the private sector. This would be called upon. Paycock Container Properties also received the Council's unanimous endorsement (discounting the woman) of its solution to the problem of cash-flow: that the packs of defaulting buyers should be repossessed.

Thus it was a particularly satisfactory meeting. Businessmen to a man, (with one exception) they had understood Lionel's purpose in introducing his product and the matter had been conducted in the centuries-old, informal way. Lionel, glowing, announced that, after he had telephoned the factory to order immediate despatch of the units, he would treat them all to a drink. Euphoria even led him to intimate that the woman councillor also was invited.

'There is something I promised to lend a hand with. When the time came,' she declined.

'Mustn't keep you from that, good lady,' he beamed, relieved, but in the early hours of the next morning he reconsidered his reply.

Because he was sure that the whisky was not responsible. Since, in-

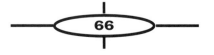

explicably, his chauffeur had gone absent, Lionel had been careful not to overdrink. His social conscience would not allow that. But from the moment he left the golf club, nothing behaved like its usual reliable self. The world had turned crazy; it had gone to the devil. To begin with, the roads were full of delivery vans — at two o'clock in the morning! — and the approach to the front elevation of his house was blocked. Therefore, in driving sleet and without a waterproof, he had to tramp through four acres of sodden mature woodland, and one of his guard dogs had gone into attack. Practically biting off the hand that fed it, he grumbled, stanching the blood. When he did finally reach his sympathetically developed cottage, he had difficulty in finding an entrance; they were hidden behind some puzzling, unauthorised extensions. Things were little improved when he entered the hall. Reaching the light switch, he discovered that illumination was nil. After a bruising journey through sun lounge, cloaks, utility room, sauna, second and third receps., he concluded that the electricity board had gone on strike, as had also his wife. A sulky flame from the last of his damp matches revealed that though she was for ever ladling out soup, she could not leave him so much as one small sample tin.

Lionel began to tremble; food in regular, large doses was essential for a man of his bulk. Perhaps a bottle, always handy in a crisis, would do the trick. It might also warm him up; he was freezing; it was amazing, the effect of soaked clothes. He had never experienced anything like this on the golf course. But the steps down to his cellar were covered with water; he discovered that as he felt it swill over his shoes and lap against his calves. Wading back, he concluded a blocked drain. Then suddenly, as he stood in his unlit hall, the thought came to him that the world in truth had gone crazy, and it was getting at him — him of all people! Someone had switched off his electricity; someone had blocked his drains; his chauffeur had deserted him; his wife was depriving him of food; his daughters and son had left. And, bandaging his bleeding hand in his scarf, he realized something else. He felt constricted. Ever since he had left the relative safety of his mature woodland and entered this house, he had felt abnormally closed in.

He recalled the strange obstacles he had encountered outside his front

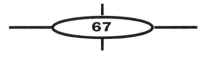

door. Inside, not a single star was visible through the windows; not a beam from his neighbour's security search-light entered his hall. It was as if he were enclosed by a dense impenetrable pelt.

The damp on his skin turning into the sweat of fever and fear, the constriction of the house finding a lodging in his chest, Lionel groped up the stairs and found no improvement. All windows were sealed with the same stifling pall. Struggling against faintness, he forced his legs to carry him up to the attic, and there through the skylight he discerned a pale gleam of stars. He rested his aching shoulders against the sill and looked out.

It took some moments to understand what he was seeing, partly because though the vision was familiar, it was also ludicrously wrong. Stacked in gigantic piles against the walls of his residence, shuttering his windows, heaped against his doors, spread in deep layers across his garden and crowding over his panoramic vistas, were thousands of Paycock Container homes, made up. 'Who is responsible for this?' he demanded aloud, but the next question came as a whimper: 'Who could have done this to me?'

He recalled his instructions to his work force five hours earlier; the operative answering the telephone had been Mrs . . . Mrs . . . er . . . a woman who owed him total allegiance. Was she responsible for this error of delivery? Nothing if not sensitive, Lionel wept.

The sleet stabbed at the containers, curling the transfers, dissolving the cardboard to mush. By the time morning came, all that remained of his efforts would be a vast scab of papier mâché disfiguring his garden and vistas. There would be nothing worth salvaging. Even the most robust, those in which he had put the best material, would not hold together when so exposed. Stretching through the skylight, he drew one to him. By now the hand that had been bitten throbbed fiercely; his whole body was shaking and his head burned; the tightness still coopered his chest. Yet none of these could hinder his pleasure in the thing he looked upon. The woman councillor had asked him to explain the offer of it, printed on the back cover of his brochure, and he had answered, 'A free gift, with every pack. It is based on a design of my grandfather's. You see, the side panels are adjustable, and therefore it can take any size. Yet it remains the most

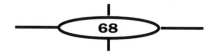

perfect of shapes.'

She had regarded the illustration of the long, narrow box, a blunt ended lozenge. 'Since you have installed no air-holes, this appears to have a rather limited use.'

He remembered that she and Mrs . . . Mrs . . . er . . . were in touch and that there had been a matter she had promised to lend a hand with. When the time came.

Lionel shuddered. He pulled the box through the skylight and placed it at his numb and swollen feet. 'Have you considered trying one for fit?' she had asked.

Her sneer distressed him; the pain of it was worse than the grip on his chest. It questioned the quality of Paycock Container products and insulted his grandfather's incomparable design. Combining beauty with functional features. Yet it was true that, fifty years ago, the model had not been tested. Perhaps, Lionel thought, he owed it to his forebear to prove its worth.

His body heavy, his brain spinning, he climbed into the cardboard casket, lowered himself painfully and pulled down the lid.

THE VANISHING OF LITTLE BOY BLUE

KIT WRIGHT

The coins were sparse.
The nights were ice.
So for a price
I bared my arse.

The wrong proof
Of blood came in.
My ashes spin
And need no roof.

My ashes spin
Above the town.
Still nothing down
For my cold kin.

A PORSCHE CRUMPLES INTO
A GREENISH FLAME,
a concave conflagration, and they run
before the fuel tank detonates, three youths
in zipper leather, and the nimble one

stops in mid-stride from curiosity
to watch a yellow tiger gut the rear.
And then they're gone breakneck for the subway,
still mad to smash things, disappear

into the underground's quick getaway.
And that is marginal. We've lost control
in a century that baffles by the need
to have possessions signify a role

or status. Breakage on the cosmic flaw,
we're nomads living just above decline,
and where the inner revolution shows
we see a divergent and healing line,

a way of building worlds in inner space,
for outwards there's nowhere to go, no beach
that isn't raked by universal trash,
dead fish, dead turtles; man on over-reach

to kill the planet. There's a place somewhere
that offers sanctuary, but it is far —
a summit in the imagination
the inward ones arrive at and a star

proclaims its liberty. Out on the street
they're sleeping in cardboard, and it is time
to rock material greed, and make of those
who sanction war and poverty a crime.

REVOLUTION

JEREMY REED

73% OF LOCAL AUTHORITIES DON'T ACCEPT YOUNG PEOPLE AS HOMELESS.

BAD DAY
MIKE PHILLIPS

Ben always reckoned afterwards that what happened that day just proved how unpredictable life can be, because he started out in the morning fed up and depressed, less than no hope, and by the evening when he went to bed everything about his life had changed.

He'd been begging down the tube the night before. Sometimes it was good. He just sat there with the card round his neck. At first he used to try clapping and singing a song but that just wore you out and it didn't seem to make any difference, so nowadays he just wrote, 'homeless please help thank you', and sat down waiting. He used to try asking them as well, but he'd packed that in after a couple of men in suits had shouted at him, pushed him over then complained upstairs that he'd been annoying the passengers. So now he just sat there. That night he hadn't got much and when they slung him out he couldn't be bothered looking for somewhere to sleep. He knew that he had to start looking. He'd been slung out of the Bed and Breakfast the day before and he reckoned he could get into one of the shelters for a couple of nights, but he'd put it off all day and now he was too tired to start walking round. You had to have a bit of energy really, because when you were looking it might take a lot of time — and money if you had it — going round all the shelters till you found somewhere. Sometimes it just wasn't worth it. Anyway, he had to meet Andrew and go down the Social Security office in the morning and if he was too far away he might get there too late or never maybe.

That was how he came to spend the night in the doorway of an estate agent's near Camden Town. It wasn't a warm night, but at least it wasn't raining, and before too long he'd started drifting. It was funny kipping out in the open like that, because most of the time you never went right off, and even in your sleep you could hear everything that went on — footsteps, arguments, car doors slamming, the voices and laughter of people on the way home. Besides, every kid on the street knew the stories about how you could be picked up and dragged off, kidnapped and murdered even. Ben was nearly seventeen, but he still felt vulnerable when he was all on his own at night and he tried to avoid going into too much of a deep sleep. So when the pitbull stood on his chest and reached for his throat he wasn't sure if it was a dream and he woke up shouting with terror, 'Get off. Get off.' He felt even worse when he opened his eyes and saw that there actually was a dog sniffing around his face. Still half asleep he sat up angrily and began striking out at it, but in a little while he realised that someone had pulled the animal away from him by the piece of rope tied round its neck.

Three punks were standing there, looking at him and laughing at his confusion. One of them was a girl, but they were all dressed in the regulation leather and studs. All of them had their hair dyed the same shade of orange. Apart from anything else, something about them was niggling at Ben's mind and when he looked at the dog again he saw that its chest and the top of its head was dyed orange. He laughed at that and one of the punks growled at him, 'What you laughing at? You're upsetting my dog.' For a moment he was worried that they might decide to round off their evening by doing him over, but the girl said, 'Leave him alone,' and they turned and walked off, pulling the dog behind them. After that it seemed to take hours before he drifted off, but only minutes before the noise of the traffic rolling down to Camden Town woke him up again. That was it, no chance of going back to sleep now, so he got up, pulled his coat round him, and began mooching down the hill towards the tube. It had been a bad night, and he was in a bad mood; cold, stiff, tired, and more depressed than he had been for a very long time.

Andrew wasn't going to arrive for a couple of hours but he sat on the pavement dozing off and the time passed quickly. In between he thought about Andrew's problem. Andrew was older, about twenty, and although they weren't actually related they had spent a few years in the same foster home. Andrew had looked after him, protected him at school and generally stood up for him, so Ben still thought about him as the closest thing he had to a brother. The only trouble was that Andrew was a bit slow, and as they got older Ben found that more often than not he was the one doing

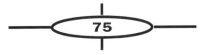

the looking after.

When Andrew turned sixteen and had to leave the home where they lived, Ben was glad not to have him tagging along all the time, but almost immediately he realised that he missed the older boy. By the time Ben was sixteen he had been mates with lots of other kids, and he was accustomed to being separated from them when he had to change foster parents or when they left the home for good. But Andrew had been his first real mate and he'd never forgotten. As soon as it was his turn to leave, he set out for London looking for the address Andrew's social worker gave him. That was several months ago. Andrew had been doing all right. Being slow he had difficulty with jobs, but usually he could live quite easily on his Giro, and still have a few bob left over for Ben. So money was no big problem until Briggs moved into the next room in the Bed and Breakfast and started stealing the other residents' Giros. He only did it once or twice a month, and he only did it to certain people, especially Andrew. Everyone knew what he was up to, just as everyone knew he was a dealer, but when Andrew confronted him he only laughed. The man who ran the hotel wouldn't do anything. He said it wasn't his business, and after a while Andrew was at his wit's end. Briggs wasn't all that big and Andrew could have beaten him up easily, as Ben suggested, but he was gentle by nature and he wouldn't. So he'd decided to ask the social security to let him collect his Giro at the office. Ben knew it would be no use, but he'd agreed to meet Andrew there and help him argue his case.

The office was just about to open and Andrew still hadn't arrived when Ben saw the girl. She was standing across the road talking to a couple of gothics, and Ben noticed her because she was different. She was dressed in jeans and a white shirt, and next to the other two she looked like a normal sixth former or a student maybe. Sort of ordinary, but she was pretty and she had a kind of irrepressible cheerfulness about her. The other thing he noticed was that she was mixed race, like him.

As Ben watched, the gothics began walking away and the girl turned to cross the road. For some reason he didn't want her to see him sitting there like an old tramp and he got up hurriedly. Someone had dropped a couple of pound coins in front of him while he slept, so he picked them up, took off his coat, and ran his hand over his hair. He was wearing jeans and a sweater and he thought that he might be looking a bit rough but not too bad. He propped himself against the wall casually and as she came past he smiled and nodded, and to his surprise she gave him a big friendly grin right back.

Ben leaned on the wall, dazed, then kicked himself for being an idiot. She must be at least eighteen if she was going to sign on, and while he had no experience with girls, he knew well enough that she wouldn't be interested in a sixteen year old, who lived like he did, on the street. On the other hand, she had given him a smile that showed she liked him and besides he was nearly seventeen. Perhaps he should try and talk to her. There had been other mixed race kids at the home, but somehow he'd never teamed up with them. The funny thing was that, now, seeing the girl, he felt an intense curiosity about who she was and where she'd come from.

He was still trying to decide what to do when Andrew arrived. He was in one of his moods, panicky and touchy at the same time. He was wearing a tightly belted raincoat and his long straggly brown hair was neatly brushed (the way their foster mother had taught them) but he had a stiff marching walk and a habit of staring which told you right away that there was something a bit peculiar about him. For the time since he'd come down to London, Ben felt a bit embarrassed about being seen with Andrew and he wondered what the girl would think.

'What do you reckon then?' Andrew said.

The question irritated Ben, although he knew that Andrew was only trying to sound confident.

'I don't know,' he said. 'Let's just go in and see.'

Inside the office they sat on one of the benches and waited. Ben could see the girl on the other side of the room, reading a book; but every time she felt his eyes on him and looked up, he looked away. The time seemed to drag on and on. What made his frustration worse was the fact that Andrew could sit there, sunk in his own thoughts for hours without showing a sign of impatience. By the time their number came up, the girl had disappeared into one of the cubicles, and Ben guessed that would be the last he saw of her.

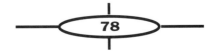

Things didn't improve. The lady they saw was kind enough, but Andrew answered her questions hesitantly and Ben had to keep on explaining. In the end she was talking to him, and Ben had to keep reminding her that it was Andrew who had the problem. It didn't seem to bother Andrew but Ben was embarrassed for him, and after all that, she said that there wasn't anything she could do right away. They'd have to send another Giro, and see what happened. Then Andrew would have to come back. It would take time. She made them fill in a form, but Ben had the feeling it wouldn't do any good.

'What do you reckon then?' Andrew said as they came out of the door.

In reply, Ben nearly shouted at him. For some reason he felt angry. Angry with Andrew for letting himself be ripped off, angry with the Social for being so useless, angry with himself for being who he was and where he was. But he'd learned long ago not to take it out on Andrew. Andrew never got angry in return, never fought back, and he always ended up feeling worse. So he took a deep breath and got a grip on himself.

'I'll walk down the bus-stop with you,' he said.

It was the only way. Normally they'd stop and have a cup of tea or something, but he knew that if they did, Andrew would keep on and on, and he'd end up getting angrier and angrier.

'What do you reckon then?' Andrew said, as they walked round the corner.

Ben was just working out what to tell him, when he saw the girl again. She was near the bus-stop and she was standing by a parked car talking to a man who was leaning out of the driver's seat. For a moment Ben was surprised. She hadn't looked desperate enough to start going with blokes cruising, but by now he knew enough about life to be realistic, and he was about to turn away because he didn't want to see her get in the car, when it struck him that there was something else going on. The girl had moved away, but almost immediately the man had got out, leaving the door open, moved across the pavement and begun pulling her towards the car.

'Shut up a minute, Andrew,' Ben said.

The street was a quiet one. There was an old couple at the bus-stop but they were looking straight ahead, minding their own business, and Ben knew that whatever was happening, the odds were that it would happen without any interfering. Somehow he knew the girl was in trouble, but he also knew that he shouldn't interfere. That was something he'd learned long before he could remember learning anything. Don't interfere. Mind your own business. On the other hand, Ben hated to see anyone being bullied or pushed around and he'd always been the one who stood up for the younger kids.

He hadn't intended to do so, but he found himself walking past the bus-stop and going straight up to the struggling couple.

'Leave her alone,' he said.

The man looked round without letting go of the girl, who was still trying to wrench away from him. He was not much older than Andrew, but he had a crewcut and he looked tough, like an off-duty soldier.

'She's my sister,' he said. 'I'm taking her home.'

But you're a white man, Ben thought, then he realised, feeling like an idiot, that it could easily be.

'He isn't,' the girl said. 'Let me go.'

'He's not your brother?' Ben asked her. He felt a bit stupid. The matter was obviously more complicated than he'd thought and perhaps he was making a fool of himself; but he knew that if you kept talking long enough people would usually calm down and sort things out.

'He is,' the girl said, 'but I'm not going home with him.'

'Go on,' Ben said. 'Let her go.'

He moved to stand between them and the car. Out of the corner of his eye he could see Andrew at the bus-stop, looking straight at him, but without any expression. Then the man let the girl go and came close to Ben. He put his face up to Ben's and stared into his eyes without saying anything. Ben stared back. The man's eyes were a greyish blue and something about them made Ben feel weak inside. Then he turned away and looked at the girl.

'All right,' he said. 'This is what you want? You want to stay in this shite?'

'Leave me alone,' the girl said in a tone so intense that it was venomous. ' Leave me alone or I'll tell someone, I mean it.'

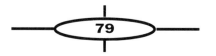

The man gave her a long angry stare, then turned back and pushed Ben aside, as if to get into the car, but instead of getting in he hit out at Ben, catching him square in the face. Ben had been hit before, but the man had caught him by surprise and he found himself on the pavement without knowing how he'd got there. There was some shouting and he heard the car drive away, then the girl was bending over him.

'Are you all right?'

Ben sat up. He shook his head, trying to work out what had happened.

'I'm sorry,' the girl said. 'It was my fault.'

'What happened?' Ben asked her.

'Your friend stopped him,' she said.

Ben felt Andrew pulling him to his feet.

'The bus,' Andrew said. 'The bus is coming.'

Even in his dizzy state Ben felt relieved. If he could get Andrew on the bus then he could talk to the girl on his own. He'd just met her now, and he could explain about Andrew in his own time.

'Quick,' he said. 'Get on it and I'll come round later.'

Andrew hesitated and he pushed him towards the stop. 'Go on.'

Ben could see Andrew looking back with a worried expression as he got on to the platform, and for one instant he felt a twinge of shame at being so eager to get rid of him, but in a few more seconds the bus had gone and he was standing on the pavement with the girl, who was still looking anxiously at him.

'Fancy a cup of tea?' he said casually.

They went into the nearest cafe. Ben knew that some of the people there must have seen the fight, but no one said anything.

'You never even said thank you to that bloke,' the girl said.

It was true, he hadn't, and when she said that he realised how it looked.

'I'll see him later,' he said. 'What was all that about? Is that geezer really your brother?'

'I don't want to talk about him,' she said. 'Tell me about yourself.'

Ben shrugged. 'Nothing much to tell,' he said. But in another moment he found himself telling her about Andrew and how they'd been fostered together and then lived in the home. After that he told her about his

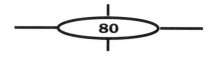

mother and how, at the age of seven, he'd run off trying to find her. She listened carefully. He couldn't remember anyone listening to him with so much attention and sympathy before — except for Andrew — but this was different. Her eyes were grey, unusual for a black person. He corrected himself, mixed, and, like her brother being white, he knew it could easily be. She interrupted once, to tell him her name, Ollie. It was unusual, short for something else, but he liked it. He liked everything about her. He couldn't quite explain why he was telling her things he had never told anyone else (he was a person who mostly kept to himself, a bit of a loner, he thought) but he had liked Ollie from the first moment he saw her, and he wanted to be friends. He hadn't made any friends since he'd been on the road. Not real friends, because it was all cliques. You had to hang out with them and do what they wanted, and with the kids he'd met so far, he hadn't been bothered. But this was different. You have to give to get, his last foster mother used to say. Be more open, Ben, if you want people to like you; and he'd known for a long time that was true, except that with most people he hadn't been bothered. Somehow with Ollie he wanted to put himself out, make her think he was special.

They'd had several cups of tea between them when she suggested going for a walk, so they strolled down to Regent's Park and sat on a bench in the afternoon sun. She began talking about herself. She came from Leicester where she'd grown up. She had a small family, her mother and her brother, who was the man he'd fought with. They were different, because they had different fathers. She wanted to be an actress, and she hadn't got into any of the courses she'd applied to, so she'd come down to London to stay in a squat round Kentish Town with a friend of a friend. To try her luck. Her mother didn't mind, but her brother was a bit mad.

Listening to her, Ben felt a little embarrassed because he hadn't passed any exams and he had no idea what he wanted to do. So he just listened.

'It's nice talking to you,' she said suddenly. 'It's not that we're that much alike, but I don't have to explain all that about my parents and everything.'

Ben knew what she meant. Normally, with other kids, when you met them on the street like this you didn't say too much about yourself. But the fact that they both had the same kind of parents, and that he had come to help

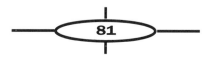

her without thinking about it, had set up a trust between them which made it easy. Even so, what she'd already told Ben just made him want to know more about her. He wanted to know what it was like growing up with her real mother the way she had. But before he could think how he wanted to say it, she looked at her watch and said she had to go. The thought threw Ben into a panic.

'It's early,' he said desperately. 'Do you want to meet up later?'

'I'm going to Brighton,' Ollie said.

Ben's panic increased. People came and went. If she went to Brighton he might never find her again.

'You don't have to go today. I was thinking we could meet up and do something.'

Ollie smiled. 'That would be nice, but I said I'd leave soon, and with my brother knowing where I am, I'd better go now. I've got some friends in Brighton.'

'You don't have to go all that way. If your brother comes back you ought just to tell him. You're grown up. He can't tell you what to do.'

'It's more complicated than that.'

Suddenly Ben remembered what she'd said to her brother, and in a flash he understood what it was all about. There'd been a girl in the hostel who had used the same word about her life at home. Complicated. He'd known what had happened to her, and somehow he knew that Ollie's story was the same.

'I know what happened,' Ben said. 'But you can't let him chase you around.'

'What do you mean, you know?' Ollie said. She sounded angry and she stared straight at him, her eyes narrowed, as if she was trying to read his thoughts.

'I don't know,' Ben mumbled. 'I thought . . . I just know.'

She continued staring at him, and suddenly Ben took his courage in both hands. If she went now he would never see her again. This was his only chance. So he said something he had occasionally imagined saying to a girl, but somehow never thought he would.

'I do like you a lot. I've never met anyone I liked so much.'

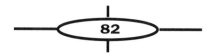

BAD DAY

He looked away from her and down at the ground. He felt her make an odd movement and when he looked round she had her face in her hands and he could tell she was crying. Ben didn't know what to do for a moment, then he put his arms round her, and to his surprise she turned round and hugged him, her body heaving, her face pressed into his sweater. The thought passed through Ben's mind that he must be a bit smelly, but she didn't seem to notice.

'I know he can't tell me what to do, but I know what he wants and I just can't face him, I can't cope with all that any more.'

Ben didn't know what he said. He was just muttering things like 'OK' and 'don't worry'.

Thinking about it later, it struck him that she must have already been a bit disturbed by being on her own in London. On top of that was the shock of what had happened with her brother. The way she broke down was no surprise. The awful thing was that he was supposed to be comforting her but he had an erection, and he was terrified that she would notice. In a little while, though, she pulled away from him, blew her nose and wiped her eyes.

'I'm sorry,' she said. 'I've never told anyone.'

'Try and forget about it,' Ben advised her. That was what they'd told him when his mother died, and he supposed that was what you had to do with that kind of trouble, because there didn't seem to be any alternative.

'Why don't you come to Brighton with me?' Ollie said.

Ben hadn't thought about it, but it seemed like a good idea. Now she'd said it, Ollie seemed thrilled by the thought. Her eyes shone and she was smiling; and Ben knew he'd go anywhere with her.

'What would your friends say?'

'They won't mind for a night or two. Then we can decide what to do. We can take the train tonight.'

The thought of taking the train stopped Ben in his tracks. He had no money and getting some would take time. There was no way he wanted Ollie to know that he begged money, and he certainly didn't want her to see him doing it. Maybe it would put her right off.

'All right,' he said.

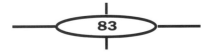

'Great!' Ollie said. She looked at her watch, 'Let's meet up at seven. In the station.'

Ben nodded. Ollie made as if to get up, then she sat down again, turned to him, took his face in her hands and kissed him. Ben felt her tongue sliding between his lips with an astonishment and excitement he could hardly control. He wasn't a virgin. He had done it a couple of times with a girl at the hostel. But she'd done it with everyone. You had to give her a packet of fags or some money, and she wouldn't kiss. Not like this, because, as she said, she didn't want to catch their germs. This was different. Ollie was different, and he felt thrilled and excited in a way he'd never done before. In a moment, though, she pulled away from him, and got up quickly.

'See ya,' she said, and she was gone.

Ben thought about it while he walked down to the bus-stop. He didn't know why he'd said he'd meet Ollie and go with her. He hadn't wanted to say no, but at the same time he knew he couldn't go because he couldn't afford a ticket, and even if he could he didn't want to be going to Brighton with someone like Ollie with no money at all in his pocket. He hadn't told her how old he was and she would be expecting him to have some money, at least to buy food. Besides, they wouldn't just be travelling together. He guessed that something would happen between them since she'd kissed him that way. Ben didn't know what it was like to have a girlfriend, but he did know that if he went with her the way he was, totally broke, he'd feel like a fool. The easiest thing was not to turn up, let her go without him, but he knew also that he couldn't do that. He couldn't miss this chance. If he worked it right they could stay together for a bit, maybe get a place of their own. He thought about the feel of Ollie's body when she'd put her arms round him and he took a deep breath. It was once in a lifetime and he knew that he might never find someone like her again. Go for it, he thought. Go for it.

The bus took the last of his money, but by the time he got down to Paddington where Andrew's Bed and Breakfast was, he had begun to work out a plan.

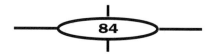

Andrew was sitting on the bed, reading a comic. The room was neat and fairly clean, but Andrew didn't have posters and stuff like that up. Instead, there were these piles of comics carefully stacked. He got one or two new ones every week and in between he would read them all over again.

'I'll tell you what I reckon,' Ben said, although Andrew hadn't asked. He sensed that Andrew was being a bit surly, for him, because he could feel that Ben was different somehow. He hadn't asked about Ollie, and Ben knew this was a sure sign that he understood, instinctively, how important she had become. 'I reckon you should get your Giro back,' Ben said. 'He's probably got it in his room.'

Andrew didn't reply. They'd had this argument before. Andrew knew that Briggs wouldn't give it up without a fight, and he had no intention of starting trouble.

'No trouble,' Ben said. 'But I'm fed up of all this rubbish, going back and forth between here and the Social Security and that. I bet he's got it in his room. I'll just go in there and look for it.'

Andrew looked up. This was a new plan.

'He can't get in here,' Ben said, 'without you seeing him. If you sit at the window and keep looking out at the front you're bound to see him. Then you just bang on the wall.'

All that was true, but Andrew took his time thinking about it, then shook his head. 'You shouldn't,' he said.

Ben nearly shouted at him for the second time that day, but he knew it only made him more stubborn, so he controlled himself and spoke to him persuasively. Their foster parents had dinned this into their heads: You shouldn't steal. Actually, Ben didn't like messing about with Andrew's principles, but everything counted on his co-operation.

'It's not really stealing. He took your Giro and we're just getting it back.'

Andrew considered that and then nodded cautiously.

'Good,' Ben said. 'Let's do it.'

'He's still in,' Andrew said.

He could tell because he knew the noises of the place so well. Ben looked at Andrew's clock. He still had about an hour.

'Don't worry,' Andrew said, noticing him fidget. 'He'll be going out soon

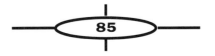

and if he doesn't, it doesn't matter.'

Ben nodded and muttered something. He wondered what Andrew would think if he knew that his plan was to rip off any money or valuables he could find in Briggs' room. Then he stopped himself thinking about it, because he knew very well that Andrew would never agree to that. But the truth was, he argued to himself, that Briggs was a villain who had made Andrew's life a misery. He wouldn't be able to complain to the police, that was for certain, because he wouldn't want them coming round and interfering. He'd never suspect Andrew, and there'd be nothing he could do.

It was nearly an hour before Andrew heard Briggs leaving his room, and by then it wasn't too far off seven. He'd have to move fast. They watched Briggs walking down the road from Andrew's window. He wasn't very big, but dressed in black leather, and with his dead black hair and white face, he looked vicious, menacing; a tough dude who would think nothing of kicking your face in.

Ben agreed the signal with Andrew again. He didn't want any mistakes. Three heavy bangs on the wall if Briggs came back. Then he slipped out of the door and down the corridor. It wasn't hard getting into the room. He pushed the door open after he heard the lock click, put the screwdriver and the plastic card away, closed it behind him and stood for a moment against the wall, getting his bearings.

It was a small room like Andrew's, but full of stuff, carelessly strewn around like a boutique at the end of a busy day. There were a couple of leather jackets, suits hung against the wall, a VCR and a Sega Mega Drive piled on top of each other in the corner. Ben took a quick look at the games – Golden Axe and The Altered Beast – good, but out of date. As he moved around he had the impression that someone was watching him, and when he looked up he found that he was gazing straight at a huge poster of Freddy, poised to spring, his steel claws gleaming. Somehow the picture made him shudder, even though he'd seen Freddy's Elm Street films loads of times; and once he knew the poster was there, those mad eyes seemed to be following him round everywhere he went in the room.

Bracing himself to ignore Freddy, he went over to the bed and looked under it. Junk. Then he lifted the mattress. Nothing except some porno

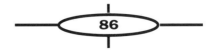

mags and a vile smell. Next the chest of drawers, full of dirty socks, shirts, underpants and odd objects like spanners, pliers, two ping-pong bats and the saddle of a mountain bike.

Ben walked round the foot of the bed, thinking furiously about where he would hide things in this place. Then as he got to the space between the bed and the window, he saw it. A black metal chest with the catches standing conveniently open. It was so convenient, in fact, that he had a brief moment of doubt. He couldn't believe that Briggs would have gone out and left his valuables unlocked. But somehow he knew that this was it, and he knelt down and threw open the lid with a feeling of mounting excitement. There was a row of small compartments at the top, each one with a few brown envelopes lying in it. The first envelope he opened had some Giros in it, the next contained money. So did the one after that and the one after that.

By the time he'd opened about half a dozen envelopes, he had a stack of notes: fives, tens, twenties, a couple of fifties. Three or four hundred maybe. He couldn't tell without counting. He was just about to stuff the notes in his pocket, when there was a sound at the door, and he looked round to see it open. Immediately afterwards, Briggs appeared.

Ben dropped the money, and made to get up, but the cramped position slowed him up and before he could do more than straighten his body, Briggs was crouched on the bed with one hand bearing down on his shoulder, while the other hand held a long sharp knife a couple of inches away from his eyes.

'You lump of black shite,' Briggs said. 'Fancy nicking from me, do you?'

Ben noticed that he had a Liverpool accent, and for an instant he wondered how long the man had been in London. It was one of those completely irrelevant things, he thought afterwards, that go through your head in the middle of a crisis.

'I never,' he said desperately. 'I was coming along and the door was open, so I just came in to see what was going on. The box was open, so I just had a look. I never went to steal your stuff man.'

Briggs laughed as if that was the funniest thing he'd heard for years, and Ben couldn't blame him.

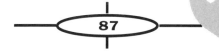

'Fucking joker,' he said. 'I'm going to have some fun with you.'

His hand moved and Ben felt a burning pain along his arm, but it was a moment before he realised that Briggs had cut him. Panic flooded through him like a wave, but he still couldn't move, because Briggs had pushed him back against the chest and was holding him there, the knife just touching his nose.

'Don't hurt much, does it?' Briggs said. 'I can do better than that.'

Ben wondered whether he was going to die here and now, squeezed in behind the bed and the window. A jumble of confused thoughts went through his mind. He thought of his mother who he couldn't remember, and he thought of Ollie's hands touching him. Under all this was terror. He closed his eyes and prayed. Don't let him.

'Leave him alone,' Andrew's voice said.

The knife went away as Briggs straightened up and turned round.

'Oh. It's you, dummy,' he said. 'Hang on, I'll do you in a bit.'

'Just leave him alone,' Andrew said. 'Come on, Ben.'

Ben started to get up, but Briggs reached out, without looking, and punched him right on the nose. Ben felt it go, the blood spurting like a fountain on to the bed. Andrew screamed. It wasn't like shouting. There were no words, just a high-pitched scream. Briggs sprang off the bed towards him. But Ben could have told him that when Andrew lost his temper and screamed like that he was unstoppable. Ben's eyes were streaming and he was trying to stop the blood flowing from his nose with the bedsheet, but he could hear Andrew hitting Briggs, a hard slapping noise. The knife clattered on to the tin box beside him. Then Briggs was on the floor, moaning.

After a little while Andrew knelt beside Ben and lifted him gently to his feet.

'Sorry,' he said. 'I went to the toilet. I never noticed him coming.'

'Doesn't matter,' Ben said. 'Let's just get your Giro.'

Next to him, the envelopes, the money and the cheques were all scattered about inside the open box, and Ben began reaching out to grab some of the notes.

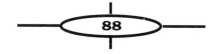

'Leave it,' Andrew said sharply. 'Leave it. It's not yours, is it?'

Ben looked at him, then changed his mind about arguing. Andrew's face was set hard, and his eyes focussed meaningfully on Ben's. Ben suddenly had the feeling that Andrew knew exactly what had been going on, and in the same moment he felt a kind of shame at the way he'd behaved.

'All right,' he said. 'Sorry, Andrew. You're right.'

Back in Andrew's room he lay on the bed. Andrew went to fetch a bandage and some disinfectant, and when he came back he fussed around wiping the blood and tying up Ben's arm. The cut was quite deep but they could see that it would heal easily, and once his nose had stopped bleeding Ben felt sick, but all right otherwise. On the other hand he felt terrible about the way he'd tried to con Andrew. Without stopping to think about it or plan how he was going to put it over, he began telling it all. How he was going to meet Ollie and go to Brighton, and how he'd intended to rip off Briggs so he'd have some money to spend, maybe get a place of his own.

Andrew listened without speaking, as he usually did. By the time Ben stopped he'd finished wrapping the bandage, and he tied it up with a little knot, then felt all round it, checking his handiwork.

'Well say something then,' Ben said.

'Why didn't you ask me?' Andrew said.

'You don't have any money, and with him nicking your Giro, there didn't seem to be any point.'

'I've got money,' Andrew said. 'I save up every week.'

He got up, felt under his mattress and took out a flat box. He'd had it for as long as Ben could remember. He kept private things in it, like a picture of his first foster mother and his birth certificate. All the kids had the same kind of secret store, which they kept safe whatever happened, and even with someone placid like Andrew, if you touched it, there'd be real trouble. Andrew held the box for a moment, almost as if he was going to stroke it, then he opened it and took out a post office book. He tossed it to Ben, who opened it and gave an incredulous whistle when he saw the amount Andrew had saved up. The dates told him that Andrew put money in every week, and he remembered that Andrew had been saving since they were

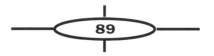

little. Even when their pocket money had been a pound or less, Andrew had faithfully gone down the post office every Saturday to deposit half of it. Nowadays he put more in. At least a couple of quid every week, sometimes as much as a fiver, and it all added up to a lot more than he'd seen in Briggs' room.

'You can have some,' Andrew said. 'Whatever you want. Go to Brighton if you want.'

'I was only going for a bit,' Ben told him. 'I was going to come back.'

Andrew thought for a long while, a tiny frown creasing his forehead.

'It doesn't matter,' he said. 'I'd rather you went with that girl and be happy. If you want.'

'Are you sure?' Ben asked him. But this time he wasn't just saying it, or trying to humour Andrew. He really wanted to know.

'I'm all right,' Andrew said. 'I'm used to being on my own, and it would be better for you than hanging about the street, being miserable.' His frown deepened. He was thinking hard. 'I can get you some money tomorrow. Tell her and then you can do it tomorrow.'

He reached into his pocket and held out a handful of change. Ben looked at the clock. It was nearly eight by now.

'She won't be there. She said seven.'

'Maybe she'll wait,' Andrew said.

He would have waited. Ben knew that. That was what he was like.

'I'll try,' he said.

There were lots of people at the station but no Ollie. Ben walked around, looking everywhere, but eventually he had to accept that she wasn't there. No big surprise, he thought; it had all been too good to be true. He began thinking about how to find her. Brighton was probably a lot smaller than London, and it wouldn't be so hard. If he slept on Andrew's floor he could get the money in the morning and be on his way. Perhaps, he thought, he'd be with her by lunchtime. But even while he was telling himself optimistic things like that, he knew that it was only a dream. Deep down he couldn't quite believe it. Ollie had gone and that was it.

Even if he could go to Brighton and find her, it would mean using Andrew's

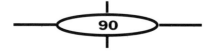

money, which he wouldn't have minded normally, except that he knew now it wasn't going to be like borrowing a bob to go on the bus. In some strange way, meeting Ollie had changed everything he felt about himself, and whether or not he found her, nothing would be quite the same again. Andrew couldn't know that, and somehow he couldn't bring himself to tell him. When he'd talked about what was going on that afternoon, he had avoided saying the worst part, and the worst part was that he had intended to go off without saying goodbye or letting Andrew know what he was doing. The truth was that when he thought about being with Ollie, and thought about maybe getting a place of his own, he had deliberately shut out the idea of Andrew, because Andrew was part of the old life, the old memories and old miseries from which he wanted to separate himself once and for all. Somewhere in the back of his mind also were the times he had ignored Andrew, or been cruel to him, or laughed at him behind his back with some other kid. There was one time at school when he'd been playing football with some other kids and Andrew had wanted to join in, but everyone else said no. No way. Not Andrew. Ben had told him to go home, not to wait, and when Andrew hesitated he had shouted at him. Later on, Andrew had been depressed and quiet, but he'd never stopped speaking or got cheesed off the way anyone else would have done. Ben knew that he had betrayed his friend's trust in him, not only then but lots of other times, and the thought made him feel both guilty and angry with Andrew.

It had been the same that afternoon. He hadn't even wanted to tell Ollie that he'd grown up with a person like that, and that he was a friend, almost a brother. But now if he took the money and went off just like that, he knew that he'd feel bad about it. Andrew would always be there, an uncomfortable secret, and he'd never be quite free of him.

All this came into his mind while he was thinking about the problem of finding Ollie. He had an idea about checking out the squats in Kentish Town. There couldn't be that many, and someone at one of the shelters would know where they were. If she'd been out on the streets like Ben it might have been easier. Most of the kids saw each other again and again, in the shelters or walking around in the West End, Camden Town, or down the squatters' club at Finsbury Park, places like that. Once you got a place

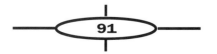

of your own or a job, you were off the scene, but if you were around a bit lots of people would know who you were and where you went usually. Ollie was too new to be known, but if he could find her friends, they might tell him her whereabouts. It wasn't a hundred per cent, but worth a try.

He walked down to the bus-stop near the station. But although there was a bus standing there he didn't even look at the number because, just at that moment, he felt a sense of loneliness and despair so strong that it made him tremble and sweat, as if he was sick, coming down with the flu or something worse. His eyes filled with tears and he stumbled across to the bench near the stop and sat down. This was it, he thought, the worst he'd ever felt, and he started swearing quietly to himself the way he used to when he was little and he was upset or in pain, 'bastards, bastards'.

After a while he felt better, enough to get on the bus and go down to Tottenham Court Road. He walked across to the shelter, and struck it lucky for the first time that day. When he asked about squats, one of the women working there brought out a list of addresses. These were squats which had been going for a while, usually with older people or students, and sometimes they didn't mind taking in kids with nowhere to go.

'There's a good place in Kensington,' the woman said. 'Have you got the fare?'

'Kentish Town,' Ben told her stubbornly. She raised her eyebrows, but she ran her finger down the piece of paper and gave him an address. Ben repeated it slowly, memorising it, then took off without hearing whatever it was she was trying to tell him.

The squat was in a road round the back of the station. By now it was dark and quiet, and as Ben approached the house he felt as if he had been walking around in a daze, as if he got from Andrew's room to Kentish Town in one of those sudden jumps you had while you were dreaming. He shook his head and began getting himself ready to talk them into telling him where Ollie had gone.

He spotted it without looking for the number. Most of the the windows were boarded up, but there was a light on downstairs. He walked up the path and banged on the door. Nothing happened and he banged again. This time a face appeared at the window beside him. He gestured, and the man

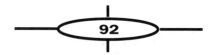

opened the bottom pane.

'What do you want?'

He had a Scottish voice, and a long thin stubbly face, with an angry expression. He didn't look very friendly. Ben took a deep breath.

'Ollie. Has she gone?'

The man frowned and glared at Ben suspiciously.

'Ollie? Who's Ollie? Don't know him.'

'She,' Ben said. 'It's a girl.'

The man laughed sarcastically.

'No girls here.'

'They said Kentish Town,' Ben told him. 'Do you know any more places around here?'

'There's another one. Up the road and and turn right.'

He slammed the window. Ben wanted to ask him the name of the road and the number, but when he tapped on the window the man pulled the curtain across. Ben banged on the window again but nothing happened, and for a moment he was angry enough to put his fist through it. But Ben knew he wouldn't come back so he turned and walked off in the direction the man had pointed. When he came out in the main road again he realised that he must have taken the wrong street and he walked back down the next turning. This went on for half an hour. Ben knew now that it was no use, but he couldn't give up. He had nothing else to do, and walking gave him time to think to try and pull himself together. He'd be going back to see Andrew in a little while, and the way he'd felt in the last hour made him think of his friend with a kind of relief. He'd always be there and he'd always be his friend, almost his brother. Ollie was a girl and that made the feelings different. But if Andrew knew he'd gone for good then maybe he'd feel as bad as Ben did about losing her. All of a sudden Ben knew that he couldn't hurt him like that. Not any more. It didn't matter how much of a weirdo Andrew seemed to other people.

By now it was dark and silent in the maze of backstreets and all he could hear was the faint echoing of his own footsteps. He turned a corner, started back to the main road, and sunk in his own thoughts, he walked past a house which, like the first one, had its upstairs windows boarded up.

He had walked a few yards past it before he noticed and in his misery he almost kept on walking, certain that it would be no use trying. In fact he had walked down so many different streets that for a moment he couldn't be sure that it wasn't the house he'd already visited. He hesitated, but it only took him a couple of seconds to realise that it was a different place, and he walked quickly up the path, banged on the door and waited. This time the door opened a crack, and a man peered out. He wore glasses, and peeping out like that, he looked like some kind of small animal peering out of his night-time hole.

'What do you want?'

Ben laughed incredulously, because the man had the same Scottish voice as the other one.

'Ollie,' he said. 'Was she here?'

The man glared at him for a moment, and Ben's heart sprang with hope.

'No. I don't know any Ollie,' he said. 'Not here.'

The door slammed and Ben leaned against the window. Now he knew that he would never find her, and he walked back out to the street feeling sick and exhausted, worse than he had that morning, because at least when he'd woken up in the doorway things had been normal, and he hadn't expected much. Now he didn't know what to do. Perhaps, he thought, going to Brighton would just make things worse. In his mind he saw all the people in all the rows of houses in all the streets he'd walked down, sitting comfortably in front of the telly, maybe eating a nice dinner, laughing, smiling, talking to each other. Then he thought of himself knocking on door after door and being turned away and he groaned aloud without knowing he had done it. So when he heard someone behind him calling his name, he thought for a moment that it was happening in his imagination and he didn't bother to turn around. Then, at once, he knew.

'Ollie,' he said. He turned around and there she was, like magic. It was as if he'd brought her to him by speaking her name, and it took him a moment before he realised that she'd come out of the house he'd just been to and followed him up the road.

'Ben. Sorry, Ben. I told them not to let anyone know I was there. He didn't know it was you, and then I saw you out of the window.' She was

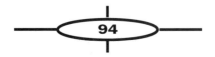

breathless, but she rushed on, gasping the words out. 'Where've you been? I waited for you. I missed the train. I thought I'd go tomorrow.'

She came close to him and he stood there, after everything he'd been thinking about her, stockstill as if he'd been paralysed, unable to move. Ollie put her arms round him and hugged him hard. But he'd forgotten about the cut and when she touched him there he winced and cried out. She felt the bandage and immediately she was all concern.

'What happened?'

It was everything he'd dreamed of. She led him into the house. The Scotsman had disappeared. She took him upstairs into a bedroom and made him lie on the bed while she unwrapped the bandage, wiped it with antiseptic and wrapped it up again.

'You're going to the hospital in the morning,' she said. 'It might be infected.'

'What about Brighton?' he asked her.

'What do you want to do?'

He considered it. He knew what he wanted to do, but he was thinking about the fact that she'd actually asked him, as if what he wanted would make all the difference. He closed his eyes. Something had been niggling away at the back of his mind. If Ollie liked him as she seemed to, and they were going to be together, then she ought to face her brother and not run away from him. He would help her. After all, if Ollie separated herself from the people closest to her she couldn't be happy. Her brother was a problem, but Ben couldn't believe that anything could be worse for Ollie than never being with her mother again.

'We've got to sort things out,' he said. 'Maybe we'll go to Brighton, but there's things to sort out first.'

That was the other idea that had struck him just a minute ago. Ollie wasn't the only one with problems to sort out. If it was bad to cut herself off from her mother, then the same was true of himself and Andrew, and at least Ollie had been completely honest. He knew now that, money or no money, he owed Andrew something, and the only way to pay it was by being honest about him, and about the way he'd tried to deny their relationship.

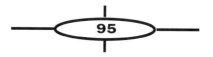

'Wherever we went,' she said, 'he could still turn up.'

For a moment he felt that she'd read his thoughts and was talking about Andrew. Then he realised she meant her brother.

'It's different,' he told her, 'now there's the two of us.'

She nodded, then she lay on the bed, turned his face towards her and began to kiss him, the way she had in the park. For a moment Ben responded, then he remembered. He wouldn't take Andrew's money, but he still wanted him to be part of his life, and he had to tell Ollie about him now, and about the rotten way he'd behaved that afternoon, or perhaps he never would. He took a deep breath.

'There's some stuff I want to tell you,' he said.

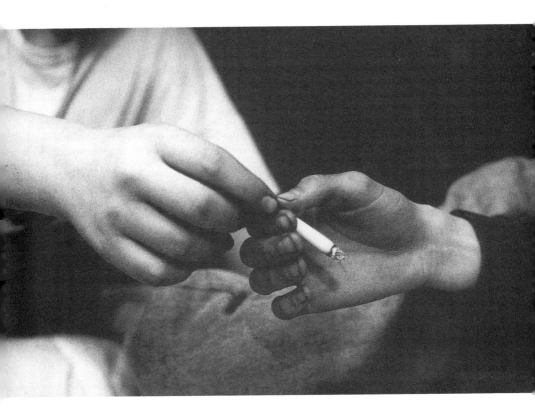

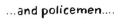
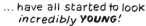

The enraged father,

His new romance on the skids,
Yells 'Get out of the car!'
The daughter stumbles out:

'I'm going, don't worry!'
But her fury dissolves quicker
Than his tail-lights can bleed
Away down the Mile End Road.

She's back to square zero.
She had her bag with her, packed.
She was happy. She was going home
And now she's not.

She sits against a door,
One elbow on the bag,
One tube of Tennent's in her hand.
She keeps telling herself to move on,

RIDES

CAROL RUMENS

But only her mind moves . . .
Like this boy she vaguely knows,
Might pull in beside her.
'How you doing?' he says.

'Fancy a drive?'
They head for the motorway.
'I hate my dad,' she says.
'All I did was tell him

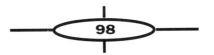

'His girlfriend's mental.'
'North or West?' the boy asks.
'Alton Towers or Stonehenge?'
She chooses North. She sings

And now she's shrieking
Upside down and his arm's
Strong and the music's loud;
Even his armpit smells good.

This is all she needs to be happy. . .
But the Towers are closed, stupid
And they put a fence round the Stones
And stoned the hippies . . .

She wakes with the sharp dawn light
Trying to get through her eyelids,
Weaving jazzy black into red
Like something to cover a settee.

Trucks are lifting her hair
On their stream. Her body's pavement:
She's got to break each bit
To sit up, to find out

If she can walk. She feels robbed.
She could have been raped, so much
Is aching, so much is empty.
She's not got a dream left

About boys or cars or fun
Because all bloody England's wrapped up,
Fenced off, there's nowhere to go
And not be taken for a ride.

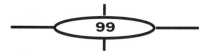

THE OLD MAIN DRAG

Shane MacGowan
THE POGUES

WHEN I FIRST CAME TO LONDON I WAS ONLY 16

With a fiver in my pocket and my ole dancing bag
I went down to the dilly to check out the scene
And I soon ended up on the old main drag
There the he-males and she-males paraded in style
And the old man with the money would flash you a smile
In the dark of an alley you'll work for a fiver
For a swift one off the wrist down on the old main drag
In the cold winter nights the old town it was chill
But there were boys in the cafes who'd give you cheap pills
If you didn't have the money you'd cajole or you'd beg
There was always lots of tuinol on the old main drag

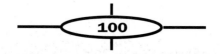

A FIVER IN MY POCKE

One evening as I was lying down by Leicester Square
I was picked up by the coppers and kicked in the balls
Between the metal doors at Vine Street I was beaten and mauled
And they ruined my good looks for the old main drag
In the tube station the old ones who were on their way out
Would dribble and vomit and grovel and shout
And the coppers would come along and push them about
And I wished I could escape from the old main drag
And now I am lying here I've had too much booze
I've been shat on and spat on and raped and abused
I know that I am dying and I wish I could beg
For some money to take me from the old main drag

ME MIND

for a buck
  id fuck ye chuck
for a pound
    id carry ye round
for a 5er or 10er
    id do as you order
for money
     ye can take me
      mind
BUT for a kind word of
    con verse
by the fire
     smoking EARTH
id show ye the
    UNI verse
id show ye
RESPECT_

Bâs
McGábhànn's
poem on
computer at
The London
Connection

BY APPOINTMENT
Jutro bedzie futro*

TOM PICKARD

After registering at the Dole I telephoned Melton Street Social Security Office and asked for an appointment.

'We have none left this week.' When I explained to the officer on the other end of the telephone that I had no money, he told me to come in and see Reception: 'They might have some appointments left.'

I tore my numbered ticket from the machine and sat beside a young woman with an exposed and swollen belly. She started to giggle. A number of old people were sitting silently; they had been waiting a long time without *being seen*. An emaciated woman, in her late fifties, gave the giggling girl a cigarette, then attacked her in a vicious cockney accent:

'You shouldn't be 'ere! I've seen sniggering faces. Come off the park this morning did ya pet? I'm not blind. You shouldn't be 'ere.'

The girl turned to face the rest of us, silently mimicking the cockney; you shouldn't be 'ere, you shouldn't be 'ere. A tall ugly man with one arm in a dirty sling got up and confronted the girl.

'Did you say something?'

She looked at him blankly, without eyes.

'Were you saying we shouldn't be 'ere?' While he interrogated the girl, his wife leered, with a red smudged grin.

I hung around for two hours while new clients came in and snapped off tickets by the minute. There was only one officer processing the enquiries. An Indian woman sat quietly talking to

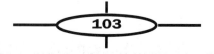

processing the enquiries. An Indian woman sat quietly talking to her young son. A smart young woman in a cream-coloured trouser suit nervously patted her hair into place. She glanced sideways at a man who watched her trying to queue-jump. She was unable to catch the attention of an official who strolled, apparently aimlessly, behind the thick perspex screen which divided them from us. Some clients indicated, through a gesture or grimace, the way they walked in or sat down, that they were there by accident. One old man said he was there on official rather than personal business. Others spoke in familiar tones of barely-concealed despair.

The emaciated cockney woman in the blue flowered dress lectured me:

'I told her! That'll keep her face shut. I used to work there. In the hotel, There's a Polish cook.'

She turned to the girl whose giggles interrupted her:

'What was the soup, girl? Salt and water? In a milk bottle was it? Where did they 'urt you?'

The girl whispered *my head*.

The cockney suddenly shouted:

'I saw you coming off of the park this morning. Is that where you're living? You shouldn't be 'ere! Your head!'

She thrust a bandaged paw into my face:

'That'll shut her face up. The bitch! I know. Yes. LOOK WHAT THEY DID TO MY FUCKING 'AND!'

The girl started to cry.

My number came up and I sat on a chair, which was screwed to the floor, in front of an official behind a thick transparent perspex wall which reached to the ceiling. While he was taking the details of my case, I could hear the cockney woman, in a gentle voice, tell the weeping girl to hang on to the packet of cigarettes she had just given her. 'They'll see you through, girl.'

The official said there were no spare interviews left and nor would there be for the next five days.

'But why couldn't that have been arranged when I telephoned?'

'We have no interviews left which can be arranged by telephone.'

'But I've got no money.'

'We can't help until you've been interviewed.'

Another number was called. The young girl was half dancing, half swaying. Her jeans were slipping, exposing her dark wiry pubic hairs. She smiled shyly. Three men, drinking beer from cans, laughed. The pensioner on official business was embarrassed, and a woman with a crying baby on her knee turned her head away.

*POLISH FOR 'TOMORROW A FUR COAT'

AT YOUR DOORSTEP

JOHN AGARD

The trees
where are the trees?

The birds
are now homeless

But have no fear.
The birds are planning
to build their nests
       in human hair

The rivers
where are the rivers?
Is this a nightmare?

No my friend
the homeless fish
are gasping
at your doorstep.
But why don't the humans
answer?

    The humans?
    What humans?

I AM MY BROTHER'S KEEPER

Or so the bishop says,
And life for my poor brother
Is getting worse these days.

You see him on the pavement,
You see him sleeping rough;
I usually give some silver:
Is 20p enough?

Imagine when it's raining;
Let's pray it doesn't freeze.
Jesus in the stable
Was better housed than these.

Yes, every year at Christmas,
The story is the same —
The homeless figures rising,
The government to blame.

A FACT AND A SCANDAL

SIMON RAE

Something ought to happen;
That's very plain to see;
The problem is enormous,
Too big for you or me.

What we need is action;
It makes me quite upset.
— Pay full tax on my mortgage?
Well, maybe not just yet . . .

DON'T TALK TO ME ABOUT ORANGES

JAMES WATSON

I. *It's snowing again*

'I keep asking myself what went wrong? Why us?'

'Us, Chip?'

'Dossing under the stars, no crib for a bed, while up the road . . .'

Chip massages my feet. Up the road, yes, it's paved with Porsches. We've been over this a dozen times. It's got to being a chant, like in church.

'But why, Sam?'

'You know the story, Chip. My mum —'

'Begging your pardon, I'm up to here with your mum.'

'But you were asking —'

'I was asking Why, not Who.'

'So Who doesn't explain Why, is that what you're saying?'

'Let's change the subject.'

I allow myself a smile on these occasions. Chip has a thought, which deserts him. Then after a quick pirouette it circles round to kick him in the bum. Not that that puts him off.

'If you go on blaming people, Sam, you'll never get to the root of the problem. It's systems.'

My turn. 'Begging your pardon, I'm up to here with your systems.'

'My systems are OK. It's other people's systems that are naff.' (True, nobody has a better system for unknotting your neck muscles than Chip.)

'OK?'

'A bit more, and down my back. Thanks.'

It's snowing again. Very pretty, really. Chip calls it Romantic. We're both frozen to death and he calls it Romantic. He's the best thing that's happened to me in two months — oh, apart from the night this drunk got

out of a Rolls and showered us with ten pound notes.

No, I kid you. It was in a dream. This drunk staggered from a Rolls. Asked for ten pence for the loos. Truth is, there's not a lot of good news hereabouts. In the dream, I said, 'I'm sorry, I've only got a fifty quid note.'

But Chip's good news.

People are kind, have you noticed that? So long as you don't try to start up a conversation. One day I went round St. James's Park, saying, 'Give us a quid, sir, and I'll leave you in peace.' It worked till somebody reported me for hassling them.

'No, it's not people who've beaten me into the ground,' says Chip. One of his favourite words is 'faith'. I think he's about to use it. 'I've got faith in people. But . . .'

We are getting round to the System again. 'But?'

'But?'

'You said "But".'

Neither of us is with it before midday; and these days not before midnight; and then it's too late to be with it at all.

'Right . . . But I can tell you one sure thing, Sam. This Chip is about to sizzle.'

The cold doesn't dampen Chip's faith. It's probably due to his circulation. 'My dad,' he says, 'used to favour cold baths. You'll have seen him in the papers — taking a dip in the Serpentine on Christmas mornings. On New Year's Day he cycled down to Hastings, dived off the end of the pier and then swam to Bexhill.'

Chip is, of course, a great liar. No, that's unfair. He is a great storyteller. A magazine I read believed that in the age of television such people are dying out. People don't even listen to themselves any more.

I listen, but then I've nothing else to do most of the time.

This I'll say, the past few weeks under moonlight and garbage have been the best education I ever had. Sure we've winos with pickled brains, who don't know if it's Saturday or Epping Forest, but the quality has gone up by the day. A couple of nights ago I slept between two PhDs. One farted all night. The other told me, while we stood for the soup, that his lab had been shut down for lack of cash only hours before he was about to discover a

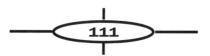

total cure for cancer.

Or was it acne?

You see, here in the lower depths you can prove nothing. If everything you hear is fantasy, what does anything matter so long as it passes the time?

Mind you, I tend to believe the newspaper that blew under the bridge this morning. It claimed that the personal income of HM the Queen increases by £1.8 million a day.

Chip and me worked out what that meant per week, per month and per year. Without bothering over the point-eight or Leap Years, that amounts to £364 million a year. Chip is for writing to the Queen with a list of our grievances and a few requests. A fresh blanket, for example. Or maybe some royal vellum to stick down our trouser bottoms at night.

Then Chip decides — no; he's got a better idea for filling the day. 'We'll present our case in person, you and me. After all, she's reported to have a conscience and she's parked just down the road.'

True, between the up-market end of Cardboard Close and Buck Palace there's a ten minute saunter. If anything, we've this superior view down to St. Paul's.

OK, so I've no other appointments. I'm stiff. Breakfast is only necessary if you're going out to do a day's work. For vacationers like us it's a luxury.

And Chip's asking me again as we come round the front of Charing Cross and head for Lord Nelson (he must be as cold as us this morning, and blinded no doubt in his good eye with all that pigeon shit), 'Why, Sam?'

And I say, 'Because, Chip.'

II. *They used to call it fainting*

We are passing under Admiralty Arch and my feet are returning from the morgue. That's what pieces of your body do — go away into hiding. You can't feel them any longer. You get the impression that the only thing that's you is the tongue in your mouth.

The rest is dead matter.

Chip says one of these days they'll send a dumper round, called Corpse

Call; before it gets light. 'They'll shake a handbell and have somebody shout, "Heave ho, the empties!"'

Very morbid, sometimes, is Chip. Actually, the others have warned me off him. He's got this temper. Very nice. Very intelligent. Well read — but very mad sometimes.

Jock never stopped warning me. 'Chip's violent, Sammy. He's got this switch-blade. He says he's used it on real meat. I believe him.'

Jock stopped warning me because Jock just went. That's what happens round these parts. Nobody leaves a forwarding address. Nobody tells you they're planning to leave.

I'm hungry now. Desperately. Joking does help; fantasising helps, but only a little. I've been wondering lately whether the best thing is just going mad.

What I suffer isn't madness, not yet; it's more like, well, like I said earlier — everything's separate. Nothing belongs, nothing connects. One thing it's not, though, is floating. No, that it definitely isn't. I'd appreciate floating.

Nothing's more real to you than the ground because sometimes, when you're really cold, really famished, the ground comes up and knocks the stuffing out of you.

I passed out yesterday and a couple of days before that. They used to call it fainting. You come round because usually there's somebody rubbing your wrists or your ankles and somebody else sacrificing half a bottle of fire water to warm you up.

If you could turn all this kindness into money, you'd be a millionaire.

'Fraternity,' says Chip, 'that's what we've got round here: alas it's one of the rarest plants in the world, facing imminent extinction. And you and me, we're practically kin — as in *kith and kin*?'

In other circumstances, I have asked myself, would Chip be someone I'd fall in love with? I decide not. Nothing really to do with Chip; it's me. I've decided the only passion that really keeps you warm is anger. Sadly, you need energy to be angry.

'That,' I say to Chip, 'is our problem.'

'Fraternity?'

'No, energy.'

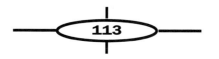

He seems to approve. I am pleased. He says, 'Now you're talking.'

'Don't tell me — it's the system.'

III. *Pussy cat, pussy cat,*
Where have you been?

These are the railings of Buckingham Palace. We're already being watched by the police. We're both filthy. The clothes aren't actually rags but these immaculate Japanese *know* what we are.

I'll say this for them, they don't betray their thoughts like westerners, like those Germans, for example, who try their best but can't disguise what they're thinking.

After all, we're sort of family: The European Community and all that.

Don't let us spoil your day, folks . . . Consider us part of the rubbish. Yes, sometimes I'm bitter.

Chip is helpfulness itself. He shouts loud enough for every tourist at the gates to hear, 'Watch out for pickpockets!'

It must be the same word in any language because the whole crowd of them feel for their pockets, grab their hand-bags, clutch their cameras.

'See that? Know what it means?' I nod. It means we're going to get moved on.

'It means we have power. They're scared. The cops are scared. You can feel the earth shake. It's scared of us too.'

'Move on, Laddie!'

Chip and I made a list last night, of the names people call us. He's chalked up 'Son of Cheetah', 'Death-Wash Six', 'Sweeney Turd', Superstench', 'Sting Rot' and — last night's latest — 'Scrofulous Prick'.

They go easier on me. I've had 'Dosserina', 'Queen of the Shite' and 'Razorhead' on account of my short hair. The worst is when they question my gender. On Monday night one of the Squad called me 'Titless'.

I've got this loose tooth — you'll have guessed my reply. 'If I'm titless, Officer, you're witless.' It was worth it to hear all the others laugh.

Still, mustn't celebrate too much. At this moment the score is, Me: One,

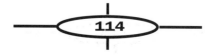

Them: Two Thousand.

We've been ushered downwind of the tourists. Not exactly into a side-street, because you can't call Buckingham Palace Road a side-street, and at first I don't think I'm hearing Chip aright. 'That wall is surmountable.'

His voice is far away, like he's under water. 'Quick, I want you to stand — that's right, back to the wall, feet apart. Great . . . Now cup your hands. Lock your fingers. Down a bit.' He tests me with his foot. 'Perfect. You could support three Sumo wrestlers one on top of the other.'

I'm feeling mind-blank again. Feet are talking to me. Feet are crying out to me — Bring us a bowl of hot water, scalding. Bring us Vesuvius or those bubbling geysers in Iceland. Bury us in the roasting sand of the Sahara.

There're no feet as poetical as my feet, especially when they are suffering. And I am thinking all this as Chip calls to me from above, puts down one arm. He used to do weight-training. I'm swinging.

'Watch the spikes — easy. Easy!'

'We must have been seen by a million motorists.'

'We're on camera, too, I reckon. But don't worry, you're in the arms of Superman.'

All at once we are down. We are down. We are running. My hand in his, and running.

I cannot describe exactly, not in detail that is, what my eyes are seeing. It's not allowed. Against the law. The Queen's gardens are covered by the Official Secrets Act.

And snow — I can definitely tell you that. I don't suppose it's a threat to the security of the realm to reveal that snow actually settles on the Royal domain.

I am hearing Chip singing:

'Pussy cat, Pussy cat,
Where have you been?
I've been up to London
To visit the Queen.

And I am also hearing a siren; two sirens. We are running. My hand in his,

GOVERNMENT ADVICE SUGGESTS THAT YOUNG PEOPLE SHOULD 'GET ON THEIR BIKES' AND MOVE TO FIND WORK. WHEN THEY DO, THEY OFTEN FIND THEY CANNOT AFFORD ANYWHERE TO LIVE IN A NEW CITY. WITH NO FIXED ADDRESS, THEY CANNOT GET A JOB.

and running. I am seeing figures all over the place. Chip is screaming. He lets go of my hand.

We're surrounded, and there are knuckles in my neck.

IV. *A very important question*

There's carpeting up marble steps and some swing doors with stained-glass coronets.

'Stand 'em up, Sidney. Brush 'em down, Bernie. She wants a word.'

Chip drops on one knee. 'Your Majesty!'

It's warm. The warmth is paradise. It is a mist in my head, purple, and there's this painting of the Madonna, enthroned, with saints to her right and left, and hovering above her are angels carrying reed baskets full of fruits, and one of the fruits has tumbled down the steps.

I think it has actually rolled out of the picture because we are being offered a similar bowl of fruit. Chip goes for banana, I for orange.

'We meant you no harm, Majesty.' Chip talks as if he's been in situations like this before. 'Only it was our earnest desire to beg your gracious leave to ask a single and humble question.'

Has he swallowed the Thesaurus?

'Thereafter, we shall prevail upon your magnanimity no further.'

Prevail upon your . . . Is it the heat?

I don't have the strength to peel the orange. 'Help her, if you please, Prime Minister.'

I hear myself say, as the peel is removed with great deftness and then the orange split into segments, two of which the Prime Minister reserves for personal consumption: 'We are neighbours.'

A servant has peeled a grape for his Mistress, who says, 'Fire away, Comrade!'

'Very well, Madam.' Chip places the tips of his fingers together as though in prayer. 'In yesterday's newspaper it said that your personal income increases by the sum of one-point-eight million pounds a day. Would that be

correct?'

'I take it,' replies Her Majesty, 'that that is not the single question you really wish to ask. What you're wanting to know is why Royalty doesn't bloody well spread it round a bit. Would I be right?'

'Well not exactly in those words, Liz.'

I am not believing what I am hearing.

'Answer me this, you envious little creep. Would you — I mean, if we switched places, would you go handing out millions to every Tom, Dick and Horace with a sob-story?'

The Prime Minister is peeling my orange, taking three segments for personal consumption. I say, 'We are neighbours.'

'I take it,' replies Her Majesty, 'that that is not the one question you wish to ask. You would like to know why I do not divide my wealth among the poor and needy, such as yourselves.'

That is better. It is more royalty-like. 'What you have to get into your tiny little head is that Royalty cannot create miracles as the Good Lord did with the loaves and the fishes.'

'Is it not correct, Prime Minister, that I would be bankrupt in twenty-four hours if I expended a mere fifty pence piece for every dosser under Charing Cross bridge, every homeless family in Bed and Breakfast in Brixton, Birmingham or Belfast, every starving infant in Africa, Asia or even East Anglia — I believe there's evidence of famine in Upton On Severn —'

The Prime Minister speaks out for Upton on Severn. 'I know the MP for that constituency very well, your Majesty. It is now free of the plague and there is not one rotting body to be seen in the street, thanks to Corpse Call.'

I am having my say. At school I was good at geography. 'Upton on Severn is not in East Anglia.'

The Queen is quick to react. 'There, what did I tell you, Prime Minister? — All is not lost with the younger generation.'

Chip has got angry. 'That's bullshit, Ma'am, if you don't mind me saying, it being a Sunday. You've got to give people a leg up. That's all they need — A start.

'If Sam and me had digs, we could qualify for support, if we got support

we could keep ourselves warm, if we could keep ourselves warm we could wash off the dirt that serves as feeble insulation against the bitter weather.

'If we did that we could get dressed smart and people'd stop shaking their heads in our direction. Then we could get a job. We could . . . we could . . . we could . . .'

'Have another banana, Scruffy Prick, and then listen to the Prime Minister of Great Britain and Northern Ireland who will explain the fallacy in your argument.'

'I'm not sure what you mean, Your Majesty, fallacy.' The PM is peeling me another orange splitting into five segments, but forgetting to give me one.

'What do I employ you people for? The fallacy is that, whoever abolished the poor would have to re-invent them. Your very own words, Prime Minister, at the last Mansion House Banquet.'

Chip is furious. 'You are not the Queen of Great Britain and Northern Ireland at all. You are an imposter. There's been an MI5 conspiracy. You have imprisoned the real Queen in an iron mask.

'And you, sir, are not the real Prime Minister. People of your distinction don't eat oranges like that, bunging the whole lot in your gob at once.'

Jock was right. Chip does carry a switch-blade and it's out now. He is shouting, 'I understand! I understand everything. The whole thing's a conspiracy.'

The Prime Minister is yelling back, 'You've got to have faith!'

V. *On the National Health*

Chip barges against me. For a second I think he's going to stab me too. He is bellowing down the corridor. 'She's not being moved. Get away — both of you!'

One's the doctor, the other's a male nurse.

'You can't do this. She needs treatment.'

'And I explained to you that she'll go on fainting if she doesn't eat. No eat, no heat. No heat — over she goes. Got it?'

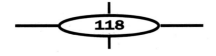

'So she'll be OK if we eat at Buckingham Palace every day?'

'Look, we've fed you both. There's nothing more we can do.'

'It's nearly dark. You should keep her in overnight — yes, for observation.'

'We need the beds.'

'But this isn't a bed. It's a trolley.'

'We need the trolley.'

'Don't come any nearer!'

'You're only storing up trouble for yourself. Please put the knife away. If you do — now — we'll say nothing. But I have to tell you, the police have been called.'

And I have to smile: where's my share of the orange, Prime Minister?

'Listen,' parleys Chip, 'nobody's more peaceable and law-abiding than I am. All I want is to prevail upon your magnanimity.'

I'm thinking, I've heard that somewhere before.

'Ejecting this young lady into the cold night is something you could regret for the rest of your life.'

'Now you listen to me.' The Doctor is a busy man. My head is rocking to and fro, now to Chip, now to the Doc, and I'm getting dizzy again. 'We've just had to send home an elderly lady who's suffered a severe stroke. That's something I'm going to regret for the rest of my life. Every night of the week people are sent home because we no longer have the means. The system, I'm afraid, no longer allows it.'

That word again.

'Was the old lady hallucinating?'

'Hallucinating?'

'Seriously hallucinating? — because this girl is. She's dangerous. You heard her. She broke into Buckingham Palace. She ate a Rottweiler guard-dog whole because the Prime Minister of Great Britain and Northern Ireland took half her orange.'

'Put the knife away please, Chip.' I am trying to get up, but flop back. The Doctor holds me.

The male nurse wishes to explain. 'We get malingerers, you see. People pretending to flake out in order to get a bed for the night.'

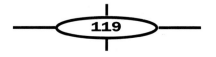

That's them; the boys in blue. Big boots, hard tiles. Four of them for poor old Chip? I've got the knife hidden under my waist. I'm sure the Doc spotted Chip shove it there, but he says nothing.

Chip's surrounded. It being a hospital the coppers are polite. 'Now, sir!'

Sir! That's a new one for the list.

Chip insists. 'I've my rights — I'm kin. All I want to do is stay by the bedside. Or rather the trolley-side.'

'You never said you were kin.' The Doc is taken by surprise. For some reason this seems to matter.

'Kin! Yes, all the way.'

'You're a relative?'

'That's what it means, doesn't it? — kith and kin?'

Which is pushing it a bit as Chip and me never set eyes on each other till last month.

I recognise one of the constables. It's Witless (and I'm Titless — joke!). He does not recognise me. They never do. Even if they come to kickstart your circulation every morning of your life they're always talking to you for the very first time.

But we recognise them. My jaw recognises Witless; and so do Chip's ribs, I guess. 'Hey, we've met!' Chip holds out his hand. 'We're the Offal of Charing Cross.'

The Doc's very small; the Cops are very tall. Somehow I think this makes a difference. He fears what they'll do to Chip once they're outside in the dark. I don't think he wants the same to happen to me.

'The girl will be staying overnight, Officer. She's been hallucinating. Could be withdrawal symptoms.'

'Junkies too?'

'NO!' That's me. What I object to is the word 'too': Junkies too. 'Just homeless. Like your daughter might be one day.'

The officer nods. 'True.' People can be very kind. 'But it's not my job to change things.'

'You can't beat the system, eh, Officer?' There is actually some communicating going on here until Chip adds, 'Well that's a problem the Queen has too.'

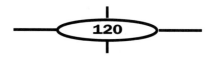

Hospital food hasn't done me so much good. Eating on an empty stomach, well, you've got to be careful. The lining shrinks and the old tum forgets what it's supposed to do, like digest. I think I'm going to vomit.

I do, over myself. I'll need cleaning up. Chip is furious.'You've scared her. That —' he points at the vomit; he doesn't really know what to say. 'is no hallucination.'

I am alone suddenly. They've wiped me clean. It occurs to me, I can sleep. I will not be disturbed. But then I *am* disturbed.

'I'm Barbara.' Another nurse. 'Doctor suggests a hot bath, would you like that?'

I'm hallucinating again. Somebody is actually asking what I'd *like*.

Jock's in my head. 'They want to check you for needle-marks.' Who can you trust? All I've got is sores and rashes.

'I'm the Land of Bugs.'

Barbara laughs. 'How old are you?'

(Jock: never tell them your real name or age.)

'Two hundred.' I sink into the fires of Vesuvius, spread my legs down the Icelandic geysers. I look at myself. Grief, I'm not so titless after all. I must ask Witless for an apology.

'You don't have to tell me anything about yourself.' Nurse sits by the bath. I look at her. If I don't have to tell her anything, then I won't.

'I'm a statistic.' That should be enough to explain everything. I appreciate her silence. She seems to get the message. 'I'll be outside.'

I can die happy. This mug of tea is the Holy Grail. Its contents will give me everlasting life. Well, at least till morning. My mother is saying, 'Everyone has a right to a new start.'

'But why should it be at my expense?' I ask.

Mum just says, 'It's time I had some happiness.'

This is unfair. I am asleep, comfy. There's a blanket over me. The tea still warms my inside. My skin's rediscovered itself. 'You glow,' said Nurse.

And yet here I am, dreaming I'm still under the bridge, dreaming I'm soaked in cardboard. My feet are toast but they are talking to me as if they're back under the sacking, lumps of frozen haddock.

(Jock: you got to laugh. I never noticed Jock ever laugh. OK, laugh — at least once I'm back under the sacking I can dream of tea and hot baths.)

Happiness is a cigar called Hamlet.

'Are you happy now, Mum?'

Hamlet is a strange name for a cigar.

'She's just gone off to sleep. I'd rather she wasn't disturbed.'

'I'm afraid it's a bit of an emergency, Doctor. Her friend had a rush of blood to the head. Now he's asking for her.'

Can this be Witless once more? He must fancy me, tits or no tits. If I married a policeman I'd get a police house.

'Just what is the problem?' I think the Doc wishes he were asleep. I open my eyes and see Witless plus one other constable. There's snow on his helmet.

'She's awake, Doctor. We can bring her back when it's over.'

There is whispering now. The Doctor gazes at me. 'I wouldn't want to give that kind of permission. She's anaemic, probably seriously ill.'

'What's happened?' That's me.

'It's your friend, Miss.' Miss? They want something from me. I am curious. 'He's up the railway bridge — Charing Cross.'

VI. *A view from the bridge*

Up it, under it, over it — I don't care; what's bothering me is the look on these guys' faces. I'm on my elbow, roll off the trolley. The Doc steadies me.

Oh no, Chip, spare us another Romantic gesture. 'Chocolate, that's what we'll need. Preferably two bars.'

'Has this happened before, Miss?' Two cops, two Misses.

Outside, there's transport. Back seat. Smell of meths. I'm dizzy, got up too quick. Trying to impress, maybe? Now I'm smelling oranges. My mouth is dry.

One fig will do, thanks, Prime Minister.

'Chocolate!'

'At this time of the morning?'

'Nothing else will work.'

'Is he nuts?'

Witless's companion is a bit of a Wit. 'Nut chocolate, how about that?'

It really must be something I ate. They are saying, 'What?' and I am singing to them:

'Oranges and lemons
Say the bells of St. Clements.'

PC Wit has already made his own mind up: '*She*'s nuts.'

'I'll give you two farthings
Say the bells of St. Martin's.'

We pull under the bridge, stop at the riverside entrance to Embankment tube station. There's a crowd — five police at least, waiting.

For little me.

Here's the Sarge again. 'Thanks, we appreciate this. It seems you're the only one he'll talk sense to.'

I don't move. I point at PC Witless. 'He's forgotten the chocolate.'

'Chocolate?'

'Nut chocolate,' adds PC Wit. 'Or just plain nuts?'

We stand about while PC Not-so-Witty is sent off to obtain chocolate. 'But where from, Sarge?'

'Use your initiative.'

These aren't all cops. Cardboard Close is awake and staring. They're stretching their legs, croaking; there's the clink of Blood Tingler, and now across the street cars have stopped.

Late-nighters in dinner suits. One asks, 'Can I be of assistance, Officer?' We're all mixing together. It's weird. Talking naturally as if we shared the same earth.

The toff produces a bottle. Looks like Scotch. 'All right, Sergeant?'

'If I get first pull at it.'

Mugs are produced all round. 'Somebody threatening to top himself, Sergeant? I'd not blame 'em in this weather. A bloody shame!'

'Nothing to get fussed about, sir. It's a nightly occurrence. Just another part of city life, like traffic jams.'

'These people are human beings, Sergeant.'

'Very true, sir. And now if you'll permit us to get on with the job.'

'Chocolate?' That's me from half way up the steps. I'm now really worried. Chip doesn't make this sort of thing a nightly occurrence.

Yes, if there's booze, there must be chocolate too. The woman stepping from the limo must be in the movies. I'll bet my inheritance she was never called Queen of the Shite.

'Will Black Magic do?'

I think she's glad to contribute. She'll dine on tonight for at least a week: 'And there was this frail waif of a girl, like death warmed up. She begged for chocolate. Her lover's last and dying wish. All at once there was a bond between us.'

Perhaps this is a movie. Going up these steps. I can see myself on screen. It is me and yet not me. I am out of breath. Never so bad before.

Need a stunt-woman to do the hard bits. I have in my left hand a half-full box of Black Magic. My other hand steadies me. Why am I so dizzy these days? Sarge leads. Witless is at my tail.

'The first train's in half an hour.' This is supposed to mean something.

My mind is on water, the river below. Sweet Thames, somebody called it. I'm cold, feet complaining. Oh stop it!

Witless is also scared, which means I misjudged him: he's human. 'Aren't those live rails, Sarge?'

Water. I'm remembering my bath. For some reason there was blood in the water, yet it's not my time. Did the nurse notice? I think she was too concentrated on trying to find out my name.

Through steel walls above the walkway. Almost stood on a sleeper, of the human variety. Nice piece of carpeting he's wrapped in. And with a good view up here on a clear day.

Best begging spot in London by the steps, Waterloo end. But breezy. The public's more generous on the South Bank. They come out full of Mozart and Mahler. They've saved all their small-change for the past week. If you've a dog with sad eyes, you might even get paper money.

People are really very kind.

Is dizzy worse than giddy? Can you be both? I see water between the struts. It's a long, long way down; and the girders are a long way up.

'There's your pal, Miss.'

VII. *It's simple if you don't look down*

Chip's balanced on top of the girder wall. Facing away, leaning away. Like he's hoping a strong wind will make his mind up for him.

He can't be reached.

'He's threatening to jump in front of the first train, Miss.'

Witless says this will cause chaos for commuter traffic.

'Can he swim, Miss?'

We all look down. 'After that drop?' I say. I don't know. We never talked about sport. 'But why me?'

'Because he asked for you.'

Witless says, 'We tried to get close — but he's got the knife.'

I am having to hold myself up. I could fall. So easy. That's the trouble with going into warm places. Half an hour and you start to get soft. I'm feeling the cold now worse than I've felt it all month. Courage, Sam: the talking will do you good. I am asking, 'What have I got to offer him?'

'Offer?'

'To offer!' My temper will keep me awake if nothing else does. 'We're bargaining for his life, aren't we?'

'You've the chocolate.'

'And if I bring him down, will you arrest him?'

Sarge: 'For his own good.'

'So I've not even freedom to offer?'

'He'll be in and out.'

'You'll fine him?'

'Can't say what the magistrates will do.'

'You want him down because he's holding up businessmen on their way to work. No other reason.'

'And businesswomen. Please, Miss — no arguing. Just get the bugger down. We'll go easy. I'll pay for his breakfast. That's a promise.'

'And mine?'

'OK, yours too.'

I'm scared. I don't like looking down through things; even on Brighton Pier I used to get the shakes. 'Chip?'

'I'm not here.'

'If you're not here, why drag me out of a warm bed?' He is silent, staring out. It's Siberia up here. The wind's got teeth like a Russian bear.

'Chip?'

'You already said that.'

'I want you to come down from there.'

'I'm holding up the traffic.'

'Miss, tell him Britain's going to the dogs already, without him making things worse.'

'You're holding the whole country to ransom, Chip.' He is unmoved. I'm shivering so badly the bridge is beginning to shake. 'Chip, this is daft. Are you going to kill yourself?'

'What else is there for me to do?'

'Just come down. The Sarge has offered to pay for both our breakfasts.'

'I'm not interested in breakfast. Thank him all the same.'

I wait. 'Chip, why did you ask for me?'

'I want somebody I know to witness what happens to me.'

I have to grip this girder. Hard. Maybe I *am* ill. Seriously. I'm suddenly sick of all this. 'OK, you've got your witness.'

'You want me to jump?'

'I want you to come down. I'm feeling ill. Yes, come down. Or don't come down. Either way. But I shouldn't be standing around. Not in this cold.'

He is sly. 'There'll be no breakfast for you unless you bring me down, right? OK. OK.' He is shivering worse than I am. He cries in his sleep — did

YOUNG PEOPLE EARN THE LEAST AND IN THE 1980s THEIR EARNINGS HAVE FALLEN RELATIVE TO OTHER WORKERS.

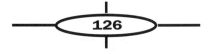

I ever mention that? I think he's crying now. His fingers are in his eyes.

He speaks without looking at me. 'OK. Are you listening, Sam?' I haven't much choice. 'Sam?'

'I'm listening, Chip.'

'I asked for you because I can trust you.'

'Thanks.'

'Trust you, that is, to tell me the truth. You understand?'

I understand this piercing wind.

'It's also a sort of test. Of our friendship.'

I thought we were sleeping partners, not friends. 'Then you can come down, Chip. Jumping's not something you should do to a friend.'

'Listen!' The cops are fidgeting, trying to whisper instructions, looking at their watches, tapping them in my direction.

'Are you listening?'

'I'm listening, Chip.' This is farce.

'I want a straight answer.'

'Right.'

'You promise?'

'Cross my heart.'

'I want you to find out something that has become of very great significance to me. Which concerns the meaning of life itself.'

He must be hallucinating. Even the police are hypotherming (Jock's word) and here we are about to discuss the Meaning of Life.

'I want you to find out, once and for all.' He is watching me now, nodding. He means business. If he does not jump, he will fall. 'I want you to find out whether Her Majesty the Queen pays taxes.'

I am flabbergasted. But silent.

'Did you hear me, Sam? You understand. You alone — does the Queen or does she not pay taxes?'

Flabbergasted but grateful: he might have asked how many angels can dance on the end of a pin. 'Is that it?'

'That's it.'

'Then you'll come down?'

'If the answer is the right one.'

(Jock: two things you've got to watch out for with Chip — his knife; and he's deep, and deep is always trouble.)

Teeth clattering, knees buckling. 'Chip, if you don't mind me asking — what difference does it make?'

'All the difference.'

I return. Police teeth chatter too. I have proof. 'What's he say —?'

'He's hallucinating.'

'But what's he *say*, what's he want?'

'He wants to know whether the Queen pays income tax.'

'No idea. None of our business.'

'Chip thinks otherwise.'

'So tell him.'

'What?'

'What he wants to hear. Christ, Lady, we're turning to blocks of ice up here.'

'I'd like to tell him the truth.'

'You want me to ring up the Palace and ask her? At quarter past four in the morning?'

Witless has spun a coin. 'Heads she does, tails she don't.'

' Chip? '

' Well? '

'The Queen does pay income tax. Like the rest of us.' Now he looks at me. I am in the fairy story when the prince has to choose from three cups — a gold one, a silver one and a mug with a Chip in it. I've thought only of myself and my cold feet, and gone for gold.

I am no longer kin. It is in his eyes. I did not tell him the truth and nothing can ever be the same.

'Got him, Sarge!'

'The knife?'

'He was going to assault the girl.'

'Thanks, Miss, you talked sense into him.' Sarge signals down the track.

They are pushing me now and they are dragging Chip. He has not spoken. It is late for apologies.

There are coins in my hand. 'Eat well, kid.'

Thirty pieces of silver.

VIII. Things're looking up

'I keep asking myself, what went wrong, why us?'

I am not so talkative these days. Keeping silent saves energy. Also, keeping my eyes shut — that helps. Not moving is even better. There is a touch of spring in the air. I may make out.

'Sam? Doesn't all this bother you?'

Sheena is my new partner under the bridge. She thinks I brood too much. She argues that there are parts of the world where people are much worse off than us.

At least, she says, we've got McDonald's.

Chip went, like Jock went. I like Sheena. She's still got spirit. She can get really angry. 'Your trouble —' she speaks to me as though I'm kin, 'is that you take it all lying down. Like you've seen and done everything. And nothing works.'

'More or less.'

She has a sense of humour. It is why I like her, why I liked Chip and Jock; why I'm not too keen these days on myself. 'OK, this one will catch you out.' What a smile, and at this time of the morning. Yes, spring is definitely round the corner.

Sheena speaks of this very original plan for filling in the day. 'Come on, shake a leg. The sun's up, there's leaves on the trees.'

She gives me a hand up. Can I feel this old?

'Did you know Britain was one of the few countries where they don't have torture?'

I don't have to answer. Like Chip, Sheena merely requires an audience.

'Mind you, that doesn't make the rest of it right, does it?'

I shake my head. In fact I am shaking from head to foot.

'So, here's the hoot. First we'll take a stroll down the Mall. Like a couple of swells who dine at the best hotels. And then, we go brazen — we rap knuckle on the front door of Buck Palace. We ask some questions.'

This time I refuse Sheena's arm. I cannot believe I have befriended two geniuses on the trot. I crash back into the shadow. All the world is suddenly old.

'Look,' I say, 'don't talk to me about oranges.'

DES RES

CAROL-ANN DUFFY

Close to the Royal Festival Hall
with lovely views of the Thames.
We recommend a personal call
soon. This is one of our gems.

Embankment (Tube) B.R. (Waterloo)
both conveniently nearby.
Use of a temporary Portaloo –
thus the price is not too high.

Charming, Dickensian atmosphere
ten minutes walk from the Strand.
A lively, colourful neighbourhood.
10ps in an outstretched hand . . .

and a cardboard box, without a hole,
perfect for single buyer.
Ideal for first-timer on the dole,
before interest-rates grow higher.

LITTLE HOUSE
IN THE BIG WOODS

little heart in skip city

all night long the wind scoops up
old leaves to keep out the cold

all night long the moon leans down
to let you lick her plate of gold

little house little heart
hold tight

TO THE
HOMELESS
CHILD IN
MYSELF

GILLIAN ALLNUTT

YOUNG PEOPLE ARE NO LONGER ELIGIBLE FOR COMMUNITY CARE GRANTS AND BUDGETING LOANS. THIS MEANS THEY CAN'T AFFORD TO BUY FURNITURE NEEDED TO MOVE INTO UNFURNISHED LOCAL AUTHORITY ACCOMMODATION.

IN REAL LIFE:
MIDGE GILLIES TALKS TO YOUNG HOMELESS PEOPLE

QUESTION: What do you do if you've been in care all your life and when you finally get a place of your own your girlfriend of seven years breaks off your engagement and throws you out of your flat, and you live in Liverpool where jobs are in short supply?

ANSWER: You get *on your bike* (or take the train to Euston) and come to London where the streets are paved with gold.

But then you find that the streets are wet and cold and hard, just like in Liverpool, and no one wants to know.

Paul, who is in his early twenties, made just such a discovery and also found himself caught in the vicious circle that sucks you in if you're homeless: you can't find anywhere to stay because you don't have enough money for a deposit (normally a month's rent in advance), and you can't get a job to earn the money for a deposit because you don't have an address.

So instead, Paul has been sleeping rough for the last nine months; finding new places to kip down with other people he meets on the streets. His first bedroom was a multi-storey carpark in China Town, which was 'roasting hot' compared with the streets outside, until it became *too* hot when security guards set their dogs on Paul and his mates.

The next stop was The Strand where he quickly learned the importance of marking out your own territory while respecting that of others:

**   *'If you try and kip down in someone else's doorway they yell at you, 'Ere this my bedroom — shift.'***

Sleeping rough means you quickly get to know the best doorways: the

deepest ones are the warmest and the most coveted.

Paul will do any work for money and he thought he'd found a job when Burger King offered him nightwork, but it fell through when they found he didn't have a bank account into which they could pay his wages. Same old story — no bank, listening or otherwise, would let him open an account unless he had a fixed address.

But now a housing association has found him a flat in the Docklands:

'It's gorgeous. I can't explain it — it's like a penthouse suite.'

QUESTION: What do you do if your mum starts living with someone you don't get on with and they don't want you there anymore, and finally they kick you out because you haven't got a job (and aren't likely to get one because there aren't many vacancies for paint sprayers in the West Midlands)?

ANSWER: You're so pissed off that at first you get into drugs — glue, solvents, cannabis, LSD — anything to relieve the boredom.

Mark, who was 14 at the time, took drugs because:

'I got a buzz from them, there was nothing else to do and it took me away from that shit–hole (home)*.'*

He left home and then returned, brlefly:

'I went back because my mum begged me to, but a dog would have been treated better than me. The last time I went to the pub he locked all the doors.'

Mark ran away again and then he heard about a hostel called The Boot

from a homeless friend (word spreads fast on the streets) and he is staying there until he can find suitable accommodation.

It's not that Birmingham, where he comes from, has a Cardboard City in the way that London does, but that, because he's young and single, he has a much slimmer chance of being given council housing than someone with a family.

And if he is offered something, the chances are that it will be a high-rise flat with a broken lift that is riddled with damp — after all, if the Government gives you the right to buy your own council house it makes sense that you'll only buy it if it's in a reasonable state. You'll leave the grotty ones for those who don't have any choice.

People leave home for a variety of reasons: they fall out with the person they're living with or they're sexually abused by someone at home, or they can't agree with the way someone wants them to lead their lives.

Take Sheila, for example. She's Asian, and finally ran away from home when she was 14 because her mum wanted her to marry someone back in India who was 20 and whom she'd only ever seen in a photo.

'I missed school because my mum thought daughters should stay at home and help with the housework. I was fed up with being bossed around.

'Looking back, I suppose the man I was meant to marry wasn't that bad, but they say you've got a choice of whether you want to marry him or not, but the choice has to be "yes".'

She knew that what she was doing would be tough for her family since girls who run away from home are seen by parts of the Asian community as loose women who drink too much and smoke dope. Sheila reacts to this angrily:

'I know why I left home and it was for a damn good reason. I haven't changed — I'm not "one of the girls", I don't have ten thousand different boyfriends, I don't drink or smoke.'

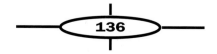

But Sheila is lucky in that she has managed to find a place in one of the few hostels for women (nationally there are nine times as many places for men as women). She's slowly returning to her Asian background, wearing the traditional dress of a charwal chemise and gossiping to her friends in Punjabi. She's also seeing her mum again.

But many aren't so lucky. Sometimes, Asian girls have had to change their identity by adopting a new name, and move to a different city where their families won't be able to kidnap them (as has happened) and force them into a marriage.

Well, OK, so some kids don't get on with their parents, but can't they find work, or, if the going really gets tough, can't they simply swallow their pride and go home for a while or get some money from the Government?

It's not that simple:

The earning power of under-25s has fallen compared with other workers, and girls earn even less than blokes. Changes to the benefit system have also meant that most 16-and 17-year-olds no longer qualify for income support, and those who can claim it are paid in arrears so they have to survive for a fortnight with no money.

And you can only claim if you produce some form of ID; a birth certificate would be ideal but that's with your parents and nine times out of ten you won't want to get in touch with them. The Department of Social Services would accept a medical card but most doctors only dish them out if you have... yes, you've guessed it... a fixed address.

Until Ken, 17, heard about The Boot, the nearest he got to a fixed address was the back of a friend's mini. Asked if conditions got cramped, he replies, without a hint of irony, 'only when the other four moved in'.

And most homeless people don't have a family to go back to, like Dave, who is 17, and now staying at The Boot after spending his childhood in

five children's homes, and with two foster parents. Between 30 and 40 per cent of people under 25 in London become homeless after leaving care.

And those who have left home have usually done so for good reason — if you know you would be going back to someone who will get drunk and beat you up or bugger you, would you go back or would you prefer to take your chances on the street?

Living on the streets isn't so bad; you don't get woken up by cars backfiring or cats fighting — you get used to that, though Paul jokingly points out that well-meaning passers-by can ruin a few good hours' sleep: *'They wake you up to give you food just when you're trying to get your head down.'* Or, less benignly, it's the police who want to search your pockets.

John, who's in his early twenties and has been on the streets since he came down to London from Scotland at the age of 15, has got used to these disturbances.

'They (the police) have got nothing better to do,' he says with no sense of outrage. *'It's obvious that people on the streets are the most likely to steal.'*

John has staked a claim to a spot in Drury Lane in the West End and sleeps under a duvet that he 'nicked from a mate'. He also has a stash of blankets hidden somewhere in Covent Garden that he digs out when his duvet doesn't offer enough protection against the cold.

But sleeping rough isn't to be recommended for your health: John suffers bouts of bronchitis about three or four times a year. Louise, who is in her early twenties, has septicaemia, or blood poisoning — a momento of the

drug culture she first discovered on the streets. She rolls up her sleeves to reveal the scars, not boastfully but in a matter–of–fact way. She's had an HIV test recently but it was negative and the close run has scared her off hard drugs for a while; now she only dabbles in hash. But if she had been HIV positive she wouldn't have been bitter.

'If I'd have had it it would have been my tough luck.'

Louise is just recovering from a breakdown. She came to London from Scotland after a bust-up with her mum's new husband and arrived penniless at the age of 14. She was propositioned by men at Euston and in her panic managed to find her way to a squat.

'I was very frightened. I was in a bad crowd and a geezer started to jack up. I began to do the same thing so I left.'

She met her husband in London Connection (one of the many places in the capital where people who sleep rough can come during the day) and they have four children between the age of one and four, but the marriage didn't work out and the kids are all in care in Scotland. Looking at the children playing in the canteen of London Connection she says quietly that she misses her own 'more than anyone can know'.

Louise feels trapped:

'I came to London for the bright lights but all I found was a frightening place. I made my big mistake and I can't get out of it.'

She spends her nights at Waterloo station with other homeless people, but her friends aren't *'real friends. They'd do the dirty as soon as look at you. Years ago I had friends but that's all changed. They've all got a bad attitude now,'* she says blankly, with no expression.

When you live on the pavement you soon see people from a different perspective and they do their best not to see you at all.
'They look down on you as if you are a piece of shit.'
(Louise)

'The men in suits, the upper class ones, they tell you to get a job —
saying you're lowering the tone of the area, the young ones stop and talk
to you, give you money.'
(John)

If you live on the streets you get to know your neighbours, you greet them
by pressing knuckles together. You're just like any other bunch of kids.

You're woken in the morning by shopkeepers asking you to move, rather
than by your mum or an alarm clock, and then you get ready for breakfast;
forming a queue outside a day hostel like London Connection before it even
opens at 8a.m., then streaming in with the other kids to get a mug of
something warm to drink. The people next to you in line wear the usual
assortment of jeans, trainers and T–shirts. Like most people first thing in
the morning they look tired and dazed.

The difference is that most of them have spent the night tucked up a
stone's throw away outside a shopfront on The Strand, against a backdrop
of traffic rushing past, people staggering out of pubs and restaurants and
the neon–lit shops glaring throughout the night. Others have spent a
restless night at railway stations constantly being moved on by police.
A day of begging, trying to keep warm and avoiding boredom stretches
ahead of them. London Connection's cafe–cumcanteen is strewn with
people in sleeping bags trying to catch up on lost sleep, despite the
constantly blaring radio, the cacophony of chatter and the crashing of
cutlery.

The walls are painted with bright, amateurish murals and littered with notices that warn of the dangers of drug and alcohol abuse, or reminders of special events. This could be any youth club in any town in Britain, but the difference is that it offers a bizarre assortment of pastimes and then the people using it head back to the streets again. As well as receiving practical advice on budgeting, cooking, compiling a CV or starting a business, at London Connection someone who has spent the night with their nose pressed against the pavement can find themselves in the surreal situation of spending a day learning how to use modern technology to compose poems on word processors; taking part in drama workshops (that reverse roles to show them what it feels like to be on the other side of the counter at a DHSS office!) or learning circus tumbling.

You can also stow your possessions in the locker room here, take a shower or strip to don a white dressing-gown while you wash your few clothes all in one go.

The rest of the day is spent in a similar way to anyone else who doesn't have a job: having 'a session' in the parks with your mates, trying to make a pint last all evening.

So if you're not so very different from anyone down on their luck, what do you want out of life? Much the same as anybody else:

Dave, who is 17 and lives in the West Midlands, wants to get into engineering, although — with heavy irony — his mates suggest that his six

'O' levels give him a good chance of becoming the next Prime Minister.

'I don't want a girlfriend yet, maybe when I've got a flat and a job...'
(Paul)

'Sex and drugs and Acid House music.'
(Nicky)

'If I had a place I could start a new life. It's all right saying we need more flats but lots of people abuse them; there should be more hostels to start with so you can get your head together — otherwise you can't hold a flat down.'
(Louise)

But with an estimated three million homeless, and of these 156,000 between the ages of 16 and 19, what hope do Louise, Paul, Pete, Sheila, Mark, Dave, John, Nicky, and the growing thousands like them, have? So long as these statistics are squeezed out of the headlines by news of fluctuating mortgage rates, the retail price index, or stories of the latest massive salary increases for company executives, Mark's simple plea will go unheeded:

'I want to sort myself out. If I could have a flat and a girlfriend I'd be all right.'

THE MINISTER OF HOUSING

Wore a telly-practised smile,
As he laid a loving finger
On the lean and empty file.

'I am happy to inform you
All our cases have been cleared:
The problem of the homeless
Has quite simply disappeared.'

And how had he accomplished
Such a record-breaking feat?
What had happened to the children
Who were sleeping in the street?

'We knew the right solution,
It just required the will:
We employed a proven method
That we borrowed from Brazil.'

FINAL SOLUTION

ROGER WODDIS

And what was it exactly
That relieved the dispossessed?
'We displayed our deep compassion,
And the death squads did the rest.'

What mattered was to hide the sights
That visitors might see.
'We must protect the tourist trade –
Another cup of tea?'

"Damn - I thought the streets were paved with gold..."

HARD-TO-LET:
Multi-Media

FARRUKH DHONDY

RADIO MONOLOGUE:

I came to hear of it from councillors. Elected members. Not for this borough, no, but they are personal friends of mine. You don't believe? Just wait. I will show you something, sir, beyond which there is no proof. I have a certificate also, but just try this first.

[THERE IS A RUSTLE OF PAPERS]

See this photo? Who is this, eh? You see. Two, three years ago. Hah. The hair is thicker, see. I bet you can't guess my age eh, sir? A little premature hair loss, that's all. When I get back on my feet I'll get that knitting thing and look my age. It runs in the family. My grand-uncle was bald from the day he was born to the day he died. They waited, but hair didn't show up.

Anyway, just have a look. You recognise yours truly, eh? Tie, collar, everything! Yours truly? And this, who is that with me? Who is it? You see. It's Paul Boateng. He is a Minister now. Very good friend of mine. I call him Paul. He calls me Pussy. My name is Purshotam actually, but they all call me Pussy. My first landlord, he started it and then the name stuck. In England, of course. In Kenya, when I was a child, they could all pronounce it and in Bombay also. The blacks, they had to say Master Damania. Some respect. We had higher rank there . . .

Oh, sorry. I'm getting distracted, but you see the proof here. I know Paul very well. In fact, I was vice chairman of the youth wing of the

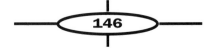

Brent Labour Party. I am still there but I don't have time for meetings. So if you can help me, I shall be very grateful.

I heard of this Hard-To-Let from some fellows I met. They were also going for it, but I tell you, sir, these fellows don't want to go about things in the honest way. I won't tell you where, because I don't like carrying tales, you know, but these fellows have gone and broken into these places and just live there illegally. They wander in and out. Mostly derelict places. Must be Hard-To-Let. They commit complete nuisance. They do toilet even if there is no toilet. Some old buggers, some young chaps also like me.

They prefer living that way. To be honest, I spent a few days with them, but I am not one of those, you see. I am not homeless, you see, I am just temporarily without any place to live. That is why I'm seeking your assistance. If you just give me permission from the council, and a flat, or anything, any accommodation which no one else wants, then I'll collect the key from any depot you name. And when I shut the door behind me, I'll clean it up myself. Even if the bathroom and toilet are smashed, I can for some days use the public. I have been using. When they open. Then when the council fixes it up, when you have the money, I can let the workmen in. My need right now is urgent, sir, urgent. And I promise, none of this bad tenancy, fighting with neighbours and all this nonsense. I am very well brought up, keep myself to myself. Clean, I smell clean.

STAGE PLAY:

ACTOR APPEARS STAGE FRONT. SPOTLIGHT CATCHES HIS UPPER HALF. THE REST OF THE STAGE IS IN DARKNESS. HE IS WEARING A SHABBY TWEED JACKET AND A GREYING WHITE SHIRT. HE HAS A TIE WHICH IS RAGGED. HE IS NOT QUITE A TRAMP, BUT LOOKS AS THOUGH HE HAS SLEPT ROUGH.

PUSSY: I don't even think this fellow understands what I am asking for.

I've tried other ways of putting it. I've tried 'difficult to let' and 'derelict council property'. He has never even heard of it. He pulls out a form and starts filling it. A policeman told me about it. These people I know, also Indians, but shameless, said to me 'bring your stuff, we are going to squat a place'. I turned up with my suitcase which I had left in the locker at the coach station. The police were already there and they were throwing out these boys who had invited me. I pretended I wasn't one of the squatters, just a passer-by, and the policeman by the van said he couldn't understand why these people made themselves intentionally homeless.

'Have they made themselves?' I asked.

'Sure they have. They came here from Bangladesh, didn't they?'

He saw the suitcase actually and a look of contempt came into his eyes.

'I'm off to the laundromat with this lot,' I said.

He said, 'Go to the council, they're having an auction for Hard-To-Let.'

The phrase has become a hope. And a terror. If they mean 'Let' when they say it, then they want cash and I'm at present in a little difficulty about cash.

Across the bridge, by Ted's Teas, four days ago, this biker lady, beautiful she was, with long golden hair when she took her helmet off and shook her head — she told me I should take a baby along. They feel sorry for babies. She was without accommodation once and the council — another town, though — gave her accommodation when she became pregnant and had the baby. Now where could I get a baby from? I know people with young children but they wouldn't lend them to me.

There's one little girl who would have been perfect, you know, but the parents don't speak to me any more. I dare not even show my face in their house. I stayed there four or five nights. He is an old friend from Kenya. We were at school together in Bombay. If you don't help old friends, who will you help?

I didn't tell them that I had been living illegally in a council tenancy and that this bastard Riaz, who was renting me the flat, had moved out and gone to Leeds when he got married. He had fixed me up with it, but I had to send him seventy pounds every month. He paid forty to the council and made handsome profit on me. Then the block closed down. The council (this is Brent I am talking about, where I joined the Young Labour Party — when I had a job I used to go to meetings) got pressurised to declare it unsafe. All the neighbours got re-housed somewhere or other, but I wasn't a tenant, you see. I got kicked out.

That was why I landed up in my friend's house. His daughter is only five years old, Yasmin. She is too sweet, eh? She used to call me 'Pussy uncle' because she thought that was so funny.

I didn't explain my situation completely. I said I'd just come down from the North and was job-hunting for a few days. I didn't say north London. I went out in the day and did look for jobs here and there or sat in the library to keep well-informed and warm. Or sat in the park. I used to sleep on the floor in their passageway, but his English wife, Yasmin's mother, like all English householders, was a bit uptight. One day I walked in and must have got my shoes mucked up in the park with dog's dirty, you know. And she made such a fuss. About the carpet and the smell and everything. You would have thought I was Hitler or something.

Then she couldn't find her Shaeffer pen one day, and in the evening I was asked to leave. So of course I couldn't borrow Yasmin.

In Bombay the beggars went around with young children singing . . .

FILM SCRIPT:

EXTERIOR. ANCIENT GREECE. A GNARLED LANDSCAPE AT THE EDGE OF A CITY. A THRONG HAS GATHERED. A MIDDLE-AGED MAN, BLIND, WITH BLOOD TRICKLING DOWN HIS CHEEKS, IS IN THE CENTRE OF A RING OF CITIZENS. HIS DAUGHTER, A CHILD OF BUT A FEW YEARS, STANDS BY HIM. THE CITIZENS OF THE TOWN ARE NOT RICHLY DRESSED BUT THEIR CLOTHES ARE ADEQUATE. THE BLIND MAN IS DRESSED, AS

IS THE CHILD, ONLY IN SACK-CLOTH. AN OFFICIATING MAN TAKES THE BLIND MAN'S HAND AND PLACES IT ON THE SHOULDER OF THE YOUNG GIRL. IN THE BLIND MAN'S OTHER HAND HE PLACES A FLUTE. A WOMAN COMES FORWARD AND GIVES THE YOUNG GIRL AN EARTHEN BOWL FOR BEGGING. THE CIRCLE PARTS TO LET THE TWO, OEDIPUS AND ANTIGONE, SET OUT INTO THE WORLD, THE YOUNG GIRL UNBLINKING, BRAVE. THEIR FEET THROW UP THE DUST OF THE ROAD. THE CAMERA CAPTURES THE SCENE FROM THE POINT OF VIEW OF THE CITIZENS OF THEBES. THEY LEAVE BEHIND THEM THE PALACE AND THE CITY THAT WAS HOME. THEIR HOME IS THE WIND AND THE SKY.

Cut to:

EXTERIOR. A POPULATED BOMBAY STREET IN THE LATE TWENTIETH CENTURY. THE STREET IS JAMMED WITH CARS AND RICKSHAWS AND BICYCLES. IT IS NOISY. THE PAVEMENT IS THRONGED WITH PEDESTRIANS AND HAWKERS SELLING FLOWERS, FRUIT, BOOKS, COLD DRINKS ETC. A BLIND WHITE-HAIRED BEGGAR WITH A WOODEN FLUTE PLAYS A TUNE. HE IS GUIDED BY HIS YOUNG DAUGHTER, MAYBE FOUR OR FIVE YEARS OLD, WHO IS DRESSED IN ABSOLUTE RAGS, HER BLACK HAIR MATTED AND BROWN WITH DIRT. SHE HAS HUGE ALERT EYES AND SHE HOLDS AN ALUMINIUM BEGGING BOWL WITH A DENT IN IT. THE BEGGAR'S FACE IS BEGRIMED AND LOOKS WEARY WITH TRAVEL. THEY ARE BOTH BAREFOOT. THEY CROSS THE STREET. THE TUNE HE PLAYS IS A FAMOUS ONE, IT IS ON THE RADIO A LOT. THE GIRL WAVES THE BEGGING BOWL GENTLY UP AND DOWN. THE TWO OF THEM TAKE UP A STATION AT THE CORNER OF THE STREET WHERE RICH CLIENTELE ARE EMERGING FROM AN AIR-CONDITIONED RESTAURANT TO GET INTO THEIR CARS. THE GIRL BEGINS TO SING THE SONG:

GIRL: (SINGS) 'Gully kohi apni, na sheher apna kohi . . .'

AS SHE SINGS, THE SUBTITLES IN ENGLISH APPEAR ON THE SCREEN:

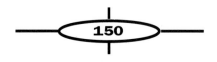

'No street is mine, no city I can call my own
How will I pass my days, and where spend my nights?
The world is a vale of tears
The world has betrayed the best
We are men of straw, men of fears
We shall never find our rest . . .'

STAGE PLAY:

STAGE FRONT, AN EMPTY SPOTLIGHT. PUSSY, A YOUNG, RATHER WELL-GROOMED FIGURE OF A MAN WITH DARK HAIR, NAKED FROM THE WAIST UP AND CARRYING INDIAN DUMB-BELLS WITH WHICH HE HAS BEEN EXERCISING, COMES INTO THE SPOTLIGHT. HE TWIRLS THE DUMB-BELLS.

PUSSY: I never passed my degree. The joke in Britain is of course BA (Calcutta) (Failed). I am actually just Bombay Matriculation failed. Didn't pass from school and then my Kenya passport was no good for remaining permanently in India, so I came here. I had some of my father's money. But it goes. So fast it goes. I spent mine on videos, one video after another in this flat. Until Riaz had taken all the furniture, the table, bed, chairs, cooker, everything except my video, and I sat there shivering and watching films.

Any bloody movie. Hindi movies, Westerns, American, English, even art movies, like Oedipus Rex and all this.

RADIO MONOLOGUE:

PUSSY: I've never made myself intentionally homeless. You see, sir, if I tell you the truth about living four years in a council flat that wasn't assigned to me, and paying the rent to Mr Riaz, then you can do two things. You can hold it against me, and my chances of Hard-

To-Let are gone down the drain, isn't it? And Riaz. I know you council chaps. You look all right and then you turn nasty. You can prosecute him and he will persecute me. He will find me and break my legs or neck. My reason for being temporarily without . . . listen, how can there be a reason? I haven't committed any sin against the Gods. In India, homelessness is a profession. If you are a Saddhu, you wander about and beg your living. But I am no beggar, sir. I am just asking for a little assistance from the council. After all, when I was working, I paid my taxes and rates. Well, I didn't pay any rates, but I am still a citizen. I've never committed any crime. She couldn't ever prove that I took the Shaeffer pen. When I said 'Jambo' to her husband, my friend from Kenya, he looked blank. The bitch must have forbidden him from speaking Swahili.

BLACK AND WHITE FILM ON TELEVISION LATE AT NIGHT:

A train crosses the bleak Russian landscape. It stops in the middle of nowhere. A soldier, a lone man, gets out, his war is over. He is going home. His uniform is torn and he carries a pack on his back and a rifle. He waits for the train to depart. He then throws the rifle away and begins to walk off. It's a gesture which lightens his load. Then he pauses, goes back, picks the rifle up, lugs it on to his back on top of his pack and begins to walk. He crosses bare terrain and then goes through a clump of trees. There is no one about.

In the distance we see smoke, and the soldier's step quickens. The chimneys of his village perhaps. A warm hearth, his family. Home.

He gets nearer to what used to be a village. It stands alone in the landscape. It has been bombed and not a house is left standing. There is no one there. The people of the village are dead or gone.

He goes through the empty streets with large craters in them where the bombs have fallen. They are not broad streets, just the little cross of a village. He gets to his own house. We get a shot of his face, desperate, questioning, not expecting this.

He gets to the rubble of what used to be his family home and finds three of the walls and the roof down. He walks into the rubble carefully as brick and dust still fall from the unstable settlement of the ruin. The household effects are still there, broken picture frames, furniture. In the corner of what used to be the front room, there is an old-fashioned gramophone, the winding type with a 'His-Master's-Voice' horn on it. There is a record on the turn-table and the needle is on the record. His footsteps on the floor, however cautious, disturb the gramophone and the record spontaneously, eerily, begins to play.

The land, the soldier, the story are Russian, but it plays an English tune:

'Oh Donna Clara
I'm in a whirl of delight
Your fascination steals my heart away . . .'

The record gets stuck in that groove. It repeats endlessly:

'My heart away . . . my heart away . . . my heart away . . . my heart away.'

The soldier stares. He might smash the gramophone, he might not. This is up to the director.

RADIO PLAY:

PUSSY: You see, sir, homelessness is the condition caused by different sorts of war. There is at first real war, then war with the

fates, then the urban struggle of our complex society. It doesn't have any one cause, but it is usually the product of human disagreement. You see King Lear, was he 'intentionally homeless'? He refused to live in his daughters' houses, castles. Why? If I was he, sir, I would have taken what I could get. Bugger pride and all this. But I don't have any daughters, at least, not yet. 'Oh look, my poor child, we need a roof over our heads!' I could have borrowed Yasmin, a friend's daughter, but I am too honest. What were you going to do? Do a DNA test to see if we are related? You would have had to take my word. But no. I played it straight. A straightforward application. Don't you think honesty ought to be rewarded? Can I go to the front of the queue on Hard-To-Let? Would you like to see the references given to me by Robin Cook — you know, Robin Cook, Labour spokesman? No?

Well, it's the movies, that's where I get half these ideas . . .

OFFICIAL'S VOICE: Mr Damania, I believe you are labouring under a misapprehension. I have taken your name down and filled in the application to get on our housing list, even though you don't fulfil the criteria. We require that you live or work in the borough at least. You don't do either. And there is no such thing as Hard-To-Let accommodation. There's only Hard-To-Get, if you'll tolerate my little joke.

PUSSY: I was told by a policeman and by a lady at the tea stall. She had a powerful motor-bike and she disappeared into the night. She didn't even bother to tuck her hair back into her helmet. She was kind to me for a few sentences. Then she went all cold and pretended I wasn't there. She must have wanted to get back to her child in a hurry. She didn't look that old either, so the child couldn't have been more than a few years, even months. She's got accommodation.

OFFICIAL'S VOICE: I know the estate from which you say you were

evicted. The other families are in short-stay on licence. Not tenancies. You people created such a fuss. Hippies and drug addicts, forming themselves into committees to complain about cockroaches. Scum against scum. They closed the place down. You weren't one of those? Anti-anti-estate wallah? Ha ha!

PUSSY: I'll take short-stay on licence. I get your joke about Hard-To-Get. It's a very good joke.

THROUGHOUT THIS INTERCHANGE THERE IS THE BACKGROUND SOUND OF 'HUMERESQUE'

[Director's note: 'Humeresque' has been given lyrics and the chorus of these lyrics is:
'Home sweet home. There is no place like home sweet home. Hearts so light and steps so fleet . . .'
This may have sentimental reverberations.]

(Producer's note to Director: Come off it. We can have the tune, but there never were any words to bloody Humeresque!)

SHORT STORY

There was a writer of film songs in Bombay. He was rich and famous. He was no longer young, but he was handsome. His hair was greying and he wore it brushed back and roguishly long, though not hanging down, merely curling up at the ends near his collar.

He was moderately successful with these love songs. He had several of them sung by very famous artists like Lata Mangeshkar. Then he wrote a song about homelessness. It wasn't a social song, about the evil of urban poverty or anything like that. It was more philosophical. He had used, as he told the journalists, like other Urdu poets before him, the idea of homelessness to

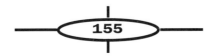

express the condition of the human soul which finds a home on this earth for a moment and then has to wander into the ultimate wilderness which is time.

The lyrics went something like this (and I am roughly translating, as the original is in Urdu):

'No street is mine, no city I can call my own
How will I pass my days, and where spend my nights?
The world is a vale of tears
The world has betrayed the best
We are men of straw, men of fears
We shall never find our rest . . .'

One day the famous song-writer, now more famous and richer than ever, goes to eat at a famous restaurant in town.

He is with friends. As they emerge from the restaurant, it is dark, and on the pavement there is a beggar with a flute, and his daughter. The beggar is playing the flute, and the young girl, in a very high-pitched whining voice, is singing the song that our hero composed. As they step out of the restaurant, the door held for them by a lackey in a uniform, the friends of the composer begin to smile.

'They are playing your tune,' says the lady friend in the blue saree.

'Not very well,' says the composer. 'Come on, let's get in the car.'

'No. Ask them to start the song again and play it right through,' says the friend in the saree.

'Give them a few rupees. That's less patronising, and let's go,' says the composer.

The beggar plays the flute intensely as though his life depended on it. The young daughter knows that there is some sort of argument going on about them, and she keeps singing, increasing the volume somewhat.

The composer's car is parked just by the pavement, ten yards from where they are.

The young woman in the blue saree approaches the beggar girl and gives her five rupees.

'Sing that song again,' she says.

The daughter stops the flautist in full flight and says something to him. They start the song again.

The composer wants to go, but his friends, especially the woman in the blue saree, insist that he stay and listen to his own song rendered on the pavement.

The song finishes and the lady in the blue saree pulls out another five-rupee note.

'What's your name?' she asks the girl.

The girl answers but we don't hear the reply.

'And where do you live?'

'Tonight? On the railway station.'

'That's enough. Let's go,' says the composer.

As they drive away he is very quiet, and his friends chatter.

'Those are the real homeless,' says the friend in the blue saree. 'You write songs about them and you are embarrassed by them.'

'They are not the real homeless. They may be roofless and roomless, but the real homeless are those who don't live in the heart of anyone else.'

'What bullshit! The reason your song sells is because Indians are sentimental and you make poverty and feeling sorry for the poor fashionable.'

'Your ten rupees is not going to buy them a house, is it?'

The other friends intervene. It's a beautiful song.

Some film magazine said, ungenerously and probably untruthfully, that he'd stolen the tune from a Greek composer.

'Funny name the girl had,' says the woman in the blue saree. 'I've never heard that before in India.'

'What was she called?'

'Antigone.'

SNAPSHOTS:

1) PUSSY HAS LIT A FIRE WITH WOOD HE HAS GATHERED INSIDE THE BARE FRONT ROOM OF A DERELICT COUNCIL FLAT. A LIDLESS KETTLE HANGS FROM WIRE OVER THE FIREPLACE, DANGLING IN THE FLAMES. HE IS CAUGHT IN THE ACT OF SCRATCHING HIS CROTCH, AS HE HAS RINGWORM.

2) YASMIN, A LITTLE GIRL OF FIVE, SKIPS IN THE SUNSHINE ON A PLOT OF GRASS OUTSIDE HER PARENTS' SECOND HOME IN NORFOLK.

3) TEENAGER WITH VERY SHORT BLONDE HAIR, CUT THAT WAY TO SPITE HER FACE, AND HUGE BLACK CIRCLES OF GRIME UNDER HER EYES WHICH MAKE HER LOOK LIKE A PANDA, IS LYING DOWN IN KIDNEY-SHAPED POSITION ON THE EMBANKMENT OF THE RIVER THAMES. SHE HAS A PROPER PILLOW. HER PERCH IS PRECARIOUS. THE TRAFFIC GOES BY. A PIGEON HAS ALIGHTED BY HER TORN SHOES OUT OF WHICH HER TOES PROTRUDE LIKE SMALL POTATOES. UNDER THE SLEEPING BODY, SOMEONE HAS PAINTED ON THE EMBANKMENT IN SLAPDASH SPRAY-PAINT 'ARABS GO HOME.'

4) [IN A BUNDLE IN THE FRONT ROOM OF THE IMPOSSIBLE-TO-LET COUNCIL FLAT] A PICTURE OF MR PURSHOTAM DAMANIA AS A YOUNG BOY SHAKING HANDS WITH A BLACK POLITICIAN CALLED PAUL BOATENG. ON THE BACK OF THE PHOTOGRAPH, IT SAYS, IN BIRO 'TO PUSSY, GOOD LUCK'. IT'S SIGNED BY THE POLITICIAN.

THROUGH THE
KEYHOLE

DAVID HUGGINS

YOUR SHOES

MICHÈLE ROBERTS

I thought I knew you as well as I know this house. No secret places, no hidey-holes, nothing in you I couldn't see. Now I realize how you kept yourself from me, how I didn't really know you at all.

You're not here any longer so how can I speak to you? You can't speak to someone who isn't there. Only mad people talk to an empty chest of drawers, a bed that hasn't been slept in for weeks. Someone half-mad, with grief that is, might pick up a shoe from the rug and hold it like a baby. Someone like me might do that. As if the shoe might still be warm or give a clue to where you've gone. One shoe pointed in fact towards the bedroom window, the view of the front garden, and the other pointed towards the door. They wanted to get out, to get away, just like you did. I made them neat again, I stowed them in the wardrobe. Just in case. I locked the wardrobe door on those rebellious shoes. They could be like me and grieve in the darkness. For a bit. Then I let them out. I'm not cruel. But they've got to learn, haven't they? Kids these days. Well.

I can't send you a letter, either, because I don't know your address. There's no point really in writing this because it can't reach you. You have to live in a house with a front door and a letter-box if the postman is to deliver mail, and I don't suppose you do. It's not very likely, is it, you've found yourself a place. I don't know where you are. You just went off, just ran out of the house in the middle of the night, and left me.

It costs me a lot to admit that, can't you understand? If I wrap my arms around myself and hold tight, it keeps the pain in. Stops it spilling out and making a terrible mess. If I keep my mouth pursed tight I can't scream or throw up. If I imagine that you're gone for good, that you'll never come back, then this terrible wailing sound will begin and never stop. I might go mad. At least this paper has ruled lines; my writing can't fall off.

If you opened the door now and came in you'd find me here in your room. I'm lying curled up in the middle of the bed, on top of the duvet. I've drawn the curtains because the light hurts my eyes. It's already lunchtime but I don't want to face the fridge, the freezer, the microwave. I'm not hungry. I'm better off here, looking at the locked wardrobe door. Your shoes are standing outside it now, side by side. The right shoe on the right-hand side and the left shoe on the left. In their proper places, no fuss, like a husband and wife. I'd like you to get married one day, I'd like you to have a normal life, of course I would. I've tied the shoes' laces together so they won't get separated or lost. White laces, that I washed and ironed.

What did you have for lunch today? I hope you ate something. Did you beg for the money to buy a burger or a sandwich? I'd like to think you had a proper lunch. Something hot. Soup, perhaps, in a styrofoam cup. You used to love tinned tomato soup. Cream of. I always urged you to eat proper meals, meat and two veg or something salady, when you got home from school. You liked snacks better as you got older, it was the fashion amongst your friends I think. All day long you ate crisps and buns and I don't know what. At tea-time when you came in you'd say you weren't hungry, then late at night I'd catch you raiding the kitchen cupboards. Fistfuls of currants and sultanas you'd jam into your mouth, one custard-cream after another; you'd wolf all my supply of chocolate bars.

How do you feed yourself out there on the street? You're too young to get a job. Who'd have you and what could you possibly do? What do you have to do to be fed? Do you have to go with men, is that it? How else could you get the money if you don't beg? There are so many of you begging for the money to buy food, stands to reason there isn't enough to go round. People don't like being continually asked, do they? They don't like being treated like bottomless-pits. These days you have to choose who to give money to. I don't mean the starving millions in Africa, I mean the people of your age hanging about outside the supermarkets and the tube stations up in London, around the railway stations, I've seen the photos in the newspapers. It's not very nice having to imagine you mixing with people like that. Drug addicts and so on. You're fifteen years old. What do those men make you do? What do you have to do to get money for food?

Your father didn't mean it when he told you those things the other night. You've got to understand, he lost his temper and used some unfortunate expressions. At your age I'm sure I wouldn't have known the meaning of any of those words. As a young girl I'd have been hit if I used such language as I've heard you use. I was very old-fashioned. Square, they called it then. I grew up in a very old-fashioned family. Of course we had marvellous times together but my father was very strict. It didn't do me any harm. There was no truancy in our family in those days I can assure you. We simply wouldn't have dared. It was unthinkable. Not like you and your friends. We weren't spoilt. Not like your generation. These enormous presents at Christmas and so on. There wasn't the money. Your father works himself nearly to death for his family, for us. Because he loves us and wants us to have what he didn't. Little luxuries. What you and your lot take for granted. And me with my teaching job, I've done my bit for you too. We've given you everything a child could possibly want.

I'm sure you'd never have left if you realized I'd be this upset. You didn't mean to hurt me, did you? You never meant to make me so unhappy I'm sure. It was that mob you got in with at school. That Vanessa for instance. I wouldn't be surprised to hear she's on drugs. She had that look. You're so innocent, you didn't realise. You're too trusting, too kind, you don't know what these people can be like.

People pretend to be kind but they're ghouls. They ring up to see how I am and I can hear them gloat. It's not their fifteen-year-old daughter who's left home and gone off God knows where. The doctor's given me something to help me sleep and I've taken a week's sick leave from school. I try to put on a cheerful face. Oh, I say: she'll be back soon, I'm sure of it. Why, she hasn't even taken her new shoes!

I don't think you have a clue how we feel. Just because we're not ones for letting it all out in public doesn't mean we don't live with this terrible pain. We don't speak of it much. But of course we know how each other feels. We have to be brave, we have to get on with living. The doctor told me: try to live from day to day. That's what they tell dying people, too. I've heard it on a radio programme on hospices. You're not to die, d'you hear? You're alive somewhere, aren't you? Sooner or later you'll ring up, won't you, from wherever you are? Some squat full of dropouts and drug addicts. Some cardboard box under a bridge. Some pile of filth. Of course they wouldn't have telephones there, I know that, you know what I mean. My daughter sleeping on a pile of filth, I can't bear it.

You've got to understand. When your father called you a dirty slut he didn't mean you to take it personally. It was just a manner of speaking. In the heat of the moment. He adores you, you know that. It's just that he feels protective of you, and he can't stand being answered back. He can't stand rudeness. Not from you, not from anybody. What did you expect, being brought home drunk at three in the morning? We were half out of our minds with worry, of course we were upset. I've always thought of you as just an empty-headed blonde; I've never thought you were really bad. Then I find out that you drink alcohol at parties and smoke pot. Of course your father was angry. After all, this is his house. You shouldn't have got so upset. I'm sure he didn't mean all of what he said.

I dreamed of my mother last night. There was so much I wanted to say to her and now it's too late.

Daughters ought to be close to their mothers. I wasn't to mine. She was a very stupid woman. She never had much of an education, then the war came and she joined up. I've still got a photo of her in uniform. Blonde hair done up in sausages on top of her head, cap stuck on one side, big lipsticked mouth. A plump woman with a loud jolly laugh. Fat, let's be honest. Terribly vulgar, always saying the wrong thing then laughing. My poor father used to wince. He shouldn't have married her, he should have chosen someone more like himself. Then I might have had a better childhood.

My mother was like you, she liked a drink. She used to do the housework with a cigarette hanging out of her mouth, then she'd put her feet up and have a gin and tonic. She was very clean, I'll give her that. She kept us and the house spotless. She never had much time for me; I was just a girl. She preferred my brother. She thought I should be a housewife like her but I surprised everybody by getting into college to do domestic science. She brought me up to know how to fill bridge rolls for parties, how to make Yorkshire pudding for Sunday lunch. Then I went ahead of her and learnt about nutritional science. Miss La-di-Da she used to call me. I was thin, rather plain. I was fair like her, but my hair was straight. She had hers dyed more golden. She had a bouffant perm. The face powder used to collect in the creases of her cheeks and melt. Then she'd powder over it. She wore a girdle to hold herself in. She lived her whole married life in a suburb in a detached house with four bedrooms and she thought it was heaven. Well, she would, after the semi-slum she grew up in up north. She was jealous because I loved my father more than her. We'd go for walks in the park together. We talked about things she couldn't understand.

It always hurt me, how nice she was to you. She spoiled you. She loved you more than she loved me. It isn't fair. That was the cry of my girlhood. I had to help with the housework but my brother did nothing. I was always racing to get done so I could go out with my father. He took me to the golf club and introduced me to all his friends. Once he took me to the pub. He told me I was bright and had a real future ahead of me. I swore that when I grew up I wouldn't be like my mother. Well at least I've kept my figure. I'm not fat like she was. She wore the most unsuitable clothes. Always whatever was in fashion, regardless. She liked bright colours, lots of costume jewellery, she looked a bit of a tart, let's face it — stiletto heels, charm bracelet, the lot.

You've got small feet just like mine. Like hers. All the women in our family have small feet. Sturdy, with a strong arch and short toes. For a couple of years now I've been able to buy your shoes without having to drag you round the shops. Moan, whine, after ten minutes in Marks you'd threaten you were going to faint and I had to get you out into the fresh air. They're lovely, these shoes I bought you. White trainers. You see I know what you like. I thought you'd love them. I'm looking after them for you. I've got them under the duvet with me now. I'm keeping an eye on them, oh yes. They are perfect because they're new, they've never been worn.

I had a white wedding. My father had been saving for years. He said nothing was too good for his little girl. He gave me away. I walked down the aisle on his arm feeling numb. I married your father on the rebound, everybody knew that. I was desperately in love with Chris, he was the great love of my life. When he went off and left me I thought I might as well marry your father. He was always there in the background, he'd been waiting for me. He's been a good husband, a good father. Everyone said how lucky I was. Of course I never told my mother I wasn't a virgin, she'd have had fifty fits. My father would have killed me if he'd known.

Of course I wanted you. Of course I love you. It's hurtful and wicked to say I don't. I suppose it's my fault you've left home to sleep rough God knows where. Go on, blame your mother, everyone else does. I'm a failure as a mother. I didn't give you enough of whatever it was. You've always been very difficult. I did my best, what more could I do? Next thing you'll be saying it's because I didn't breastfeed you, or because I didn't pick you up every time you cried. You can't imagine what it was like. At night you cried so much, in the end I used to shut the door on you and go back downstairs. I was exhausted. Your father slept through most of it; he said it wasn't his job. Just like my father. He wasn't interested in me when I was little, then when I was older and showed I had a brain, that was when he got involved. Oh, but we did have a lot of happy times too, I know we did. Don't forget that. I wish you wouldn't sulk. I wish you'd stop sulking and answer me.

It's cosy in here. Peaceful too. I've unplugged the telephone so that I can concentrate on you and we shan't be disturbed. It'll be dark soon, the street lamps have just come on. I can see one shining through the curtains. Funny, you never did like these curtains. I remember I got them in a sale up in town. I thought they were lovely, really modern with these splashes of blue and grey, they were exactly what I'd have wanted as a girl. Then when you came home and saw what I'd done you flew into a temper, you said you wanted the old curtains back. By then it was too late, I'd thrown them away. I'd gone to so much trouble to give you a surprise, I couldn't believe you'd be so ungrateful. Then you had to go and burst into floods of tears. That was the last straw. Oh you used to be so unkind to me. Throwing my presents back in my face.

At first I kept the shoes in the box I made them pack them in at the shop, tenderly wrapped in tissue-paper. Delicate white sheets, rustling, uncreased. Then I tried them in the wardrobe, then side by side on the rug. They're best in here with me I think, safe and warm in bed. Tucked uptight.

How could you do that to us? How could you? Boasting about it even. I

THERE ARE FEWER HOSTEL PLACES FOR WOMEN THAN MEN — 3,522 OUT OF 22,424 TOTAL.

think you wanted us to find out. Thank God I had the sense to look in your bag that night. You laughed at me, you said lots of girls in your class had had sex by the time they were fifteen, you weren't going to be the exception.

After my mother died I had to clear out her clothes and pack them up for jumble. Her shoes hurt me so much. Rows of big heels, all of them too small for her, she was so vain, all of them moulded to the shape of her poor feet. You could see how her toes were all bent over, misshapen. Bulges where she'd had bunions, corn-plasters. Who'd have wanted them? I threw them all in the dustbin. Then on the way home I stopped the car and bought you a pair of new shoes as a surprise, really beautiful ones, the best I could afford.

Your father will be home soon. I've locked the bedroom door so that he can't get in. I want to be alone with you for a bit. My darling girl whom I love so much. I hold you to my breast and rock you like my mother never rocked me. You're so small and pale. Let me hold you while you cry.

Laces like strings of white liquorice. They taste sweet.

There, my darling, there. You're at home with mother, everything's all right. I knew you'd come back, I knew you'd come back to me.

I love you, I love you so much, oh yes, oh yes.

LADIES AND GENTLEMEN

MICHAEL ROSEN

Good evening

To suggest that huge empty office blocks
in Docklands
is in any way linked to the problem of the young homeless
is ridiculous

To suggest that the diminishing amount of council accommodation
through sales
is in any way linked to the problem of the young homeless
is absurd

To suggest that councils evicting squatters
from unused property
is in any way linked to the problem of the young homeless
is naïve

To suggest that landlords demanding evidence of a full-time job
before letting to tenants
is in any way linked to the problem of the young homeless
is simplistic

To suggest that employers demanding evidence of a fixed address
before taking someone on
is in any way linked to the problem of the young homeless
is a misunderstanding

To suggest that difficulties in claiming benefit
and income support
is in any way linked to the problem of the young homeless
is just propaganda

To suggest that the property boom which pushed the cost of
property
out of reach of the poor
is in any way linked to the problem of the young homeless
is preposterous

To suggest that a slow-down in the building
of low-cost accommodation
is in any way linked to the problem of the young homeless
is a distortion of the facts

To suggest that
after many years of decline, Britain is now a land of opportunity
after many years of socialist stranglehold, we are now freer than we've
ever been
after many years of Welfare State nannying, young people on the streets
have got only themselves to blame
is much nearer the truth

thank you and goodnight,
(make it a double, George, I'm shattered)

ABOUT THE CONTRIBUTORS:

JOHN AGARD was born in Guyana. He came to Britain in 1977 and was attached to the Commonwealth Institute for seven years as a touring speaker. His poetry books for children include *I Din Do Nuttin, Say It Again Granny* (Bodley Head/Magnet) and *Laughter Is An Egg* (Puffin).

GILLIAN ALLNUTT was born in London and now lives in Newcastle. A former poetry editor of *City Limits*, she now teaches creative writing. Her collections include *Spitting the Pips out* (Virago), and *Beginning the Avocado* (Virago). She has also written *Berthing: A Poetry Word Book for Women* (Virago).

SIMON ARMITAGE lives in Yorkshire, and works as a probation officer. His first poetry collection, *Zoom*, was published by Bloodaxe (1991), to great acclaim.

ROS ASQUITH is a freelance 'hackette' living in London. She has been a theatre critic for *Time Out*, *The Observer* and *City Limits*, and now does the weekly 'Doris' cartoon in *The Guardian*. Her own books include *Baby!, Toddler!, Babies!* and *Green!* (Pandora).

STEVE BELL has had a daily strip in *The Guardian* since 1981, and regularly contributes to *Time Out, City Limits* and *New Statesman & Society*.

JOHN BENTLY is a painter and poet, and the maker of the *Liver and Lights* series of artists' books. (The painting included in this book originally appeared in *Liver and Lights* No. 10.) He lives in South East London.

KATIE CAMPBELL is a Canadian living in London. She writes plays for radio and theatre; her *Lipstick Tango* was performed at this year's Edinburgh Festival, and her adaptation of Doris Lessing's *In Pursuit of the English* had an extended run at the Lyric Theatre last spring. A short story collection *What He Really Wants Is A Dog*, and a poetry collection *Let Us Leave Them Believing* are both published by Methuen.

FARRUKH DHONDY is a commissioning editor at Channel 4. He is well known as a scriptwriter and author for teenagers, as well as for his novel *Bombay Duck* (Cape).

CAROL-ANN DUFFY was born in Glasgow and now lives in London. She has won many awards for her poetry including the 1988 Somerset Maugham Award. Her work includes *Selling Manhattan*, *The Other Country* and *Standing Female Nude* (Anvil).

GEOFF DYER lives in London. He has contributed to a variety of magazines and newspapers including *The Listener, New Statesman & Society, City Limits, Marxism Today* and *Literary Review*. His work includes a study of John Berger's work — *Ways of Telling* (Pluto Press), *The Colour of Memory* and most recently *But Beautiful* (Cape).

ADÈLE GERAS writes books for young adults and children, as well as poetry. She has recently contributed to *New Women Poets* edited by Carol Rumens (Bloodaxe). She lives in Manchester with her husband and two children.

MIDGE GILLIES graduated from Cambridge in 1985, and presently works as a reporter on *The Birmingham Post.*

DAVID HALDANE lives in Northumberland, and contributes cartoons regularly to *Punch*, *Private Eye* and *The Sunday Times.*

JOHN HEGLEY, comic poet, singer, songwriter and glasses wearer performs all over the country in theatres, at gigs, at the Edinburgh Festival and many times on the radio and television. He contributes weekly to *The Guardian,* and in *The Observer's* Expert's Expert feature he was chosen as the top fringe comedian.

DAVID HUGGINS lives in London and is a freelance illustrator, contributing to a number of magazines. He used to have a cockatoo called Olive . . .

TONY HUSBAND does the 'Yob' strip for *Private Eye*, and has contributed cartoons to *Punch* and *The Sunday Times* regularly since 1984. He has won the Cartoonist of the Year Award five times.

MARK ILLIS was educated at University College London and UEA. His first published story was runner up for the Whitbread Prize and subsequent stories have been published in the *London Review of Book*s, *London Magazine* and *Fiction Magazine*. Now 27, he has had two novels published by Bloomsbury: *A Chinese Summer,* and *The Alchemist* — to great acclaim. His novel *The Feather Report* will be published next year. He lives in London, and is writer in residence at Slough Library.

MAGGIE LING contributes cartoons to *The Observer* and various womens magazines. Her collection *One Woman's Eye — a wry look at life* was published by Virago in 1986.

ANDREZEJ KRAUE- came from Poland in 1982. He currently contributes cartoons to *The Guardian, New Statesman* & Society and *The New Scientist* as well as to magazines. He also designs posters — including those for The Old Vic Theatre.

PAUL MILLER lives in London. Previously an assistant TV producer on wild life programmes, he is currently studying at the National Film School.

MARYLOU NORTH trained as a graphic designer at the London College of Printing. She prefers to work in illustration, which she now combines with working a hill farm on Dartmoor.

SAM NORTH lives in London, and works for a Soho film production company. At 27 he won the Somerset Maugham Award for his novel *The Automatic Man* (Secker), which has been followed by *Chapel Street,* and his forthcoming novel, *The Gifting Programme.*

JUNE OLDHAM lives in Ilkley, West Yorkshire. She has gained a wide reputation for her writing for young adults, including titles such as *Enter Tom*, and *Grow Up, Cupid*. Her first adult novel *Flames* (Virago, 1986), was awarded the joint Yorkshire Arts Association and Virago Fiction Prize and has been followed by *A Little Rattle in the Air* (Virago). June Oldham has worked in community arts in two long writing residencies.

JACK O'SULLIVAN is the Social Services Correspondent for *The Independent.*

MIKE PHILLIPS was born in Guyana and came to Britain in 1956. He worked and lived in a hostel for homeless black youths in Notting Hill, leaving that to become a 'community activist' in Manchester and Birmingham. He entered journalism halfway through the seventies and now teaches at the Polytechnic of Central London. He has published two novels, *Blood Rights* and *The Late Candidate* — which was awarded the Crime Writers' Association's Silver Dagger Award. His next novel *Point of Darkness* (Michael Joseph) is due to be published early in 1992.

TOM PICKARD writes for television, film and radio. His published poetry collections include *High On The Walls*, *The Order of Chance*, *Hero Dust* and *Custom and Exile*. He is currently completing the editing of a new poetry series *Word of Mouth*, which he is directing for Border Television.

FIONA PITT-KETHLEY has published three collections of poetry, *Sky Ray Lolly*, *Private Parts* and *The Perfect Man* (Chatto), a travel book — *Journeys to the Underworld* and a novel, *The Misfortunes of Nigel*. Her anthology, *The Literary Companion to Sex* will be published in February 1992.

SIMON RAE is presenter of Radio 4's *Poetry Please!* and is also well known for his regular contributions to *The Weekend Guardian.*

JEREMY REED's works include *Nineties* (Cape),his autobiography *Lipstick, Sex and Poetry* (Peter Owen), and his study of Lou Reed *Waiting for the Man* (Picador). *Red Haired Android* will be published spring 1992 by Harper Collins.

MICHÈLE ROBERTS is a celebrated short story writer and novelist. Her works include *A Piece of the Night* (Women's Press), *The Visitation* (Women's Press), *The Wild Girl* (Methuen) and *The Book of Mrs Noah* (Methuen). She has contributed to various short story anthologies, and her volume of poetry, *The Mirror of the Mother,* was published in 1986 by Methuen. She lives and works in London.

CAROL RUMENS was born in South London. She has published six volumes of poetry, including *From Berlin to Heaven* (Chatto) and *The Greening of Snow Beach* (Bloodaxe). She has also written a novel, *Plato Park* (Flamingo), and is the co-translator of The *Poetry of Perestroika* (Iron Press). Um... like the extension!

ABOUT THE CONTRIBUTORS

POSY SIMMONDS studied art at The Sorbonne and The Central School of Art and Design. She is well known for her cartoons in newspapers and magazines such as *The Guardian*, *The Times* and *Cosmopolitan*. Her published collections include *Mrs Weber's Diary* (1979), *True Love* (1981), *Pick of Posy* (1982), *Very Posy* (1985) and *Pure Posy* (1987).

MATT SIMPSON lives and works in Liverpool. His most recent poetry collection is *An Elegy for the Galosherman — New and Selected Poems* (Bloodaxe). He is also working on a forthcoming collection of children's poetry.

PAUL THOMAS lives in London. He regularly contributes cartoons to *Punch*, The *Independent* and *The Evening Standard*.

BILL TIDY has written and illustrated over eighty books, and has contributed to *The New Scientist* and *General Practitioner* for over twenty years. He is well known for his TV and radio appearances. He also designs board games.

CLARA VULLIAMY trained in fine art at The Royal Academy and now works as an illustrator for magazines and newspapers, including *Men: A User's Guide* for *The Guardian*. She has had three children's books published.

JAMES WATSON was born in Lancashire. He was a journalist and now lectures in communication and media studies. He has written six novels for teenagers with political and historical backcloths, including the highly acclaimed *Talking In Whispers* which won the Other Award. He has also had several radio plays broadcast by the BBC.

ROGER WODDIS, ex-customs officer, has been a professional writer for the past thirty years. His work includes cartoon strips, short stories, plays for stage, radio and television. His published works include *The Woddis Collection*, *God's Worried* and, in collaboration with cartoonist Steve Bell *Funny Old World* (Methuen). He is a regular contributor to *New Statesman & Society*, *Punch*, *Radio Times* and *The Listener*.

KIT WRIGHT lives in London. An award-winning poet, he has been Education Secretary to the Poetry Society, and Fellow Commoner in the Creative Arts at Trinity College. He teaches poetry workshops, as well as giving readings.

"I HATE IT WHEN CELEBRITIES SLEEP OUT TO SUPPORT THE HOMELESS. I NEVER KNOW WHETHER TO MOVE 'EM ON OR ASK FOR THEIR AUTOGRAPH."

PEOPLE NEED SHELTER

SHELTER NEEDS YOUR HELP

It costs Shelter an average of £75,610 a year to run just *one* Shelter Housing aid centre. That means £80.60 for our caseworkers to give each person or family in need professional housing advice, which frequently results in preventing them from becoming homeless.

Please help us in whatever way you can by sending a cheque or postal order, made out to Shelter, to:

Shelter, Room 708
FREEPOST
LONDON EC1B 1ND

Or by sending a SAE for more information on our work with homeless people.

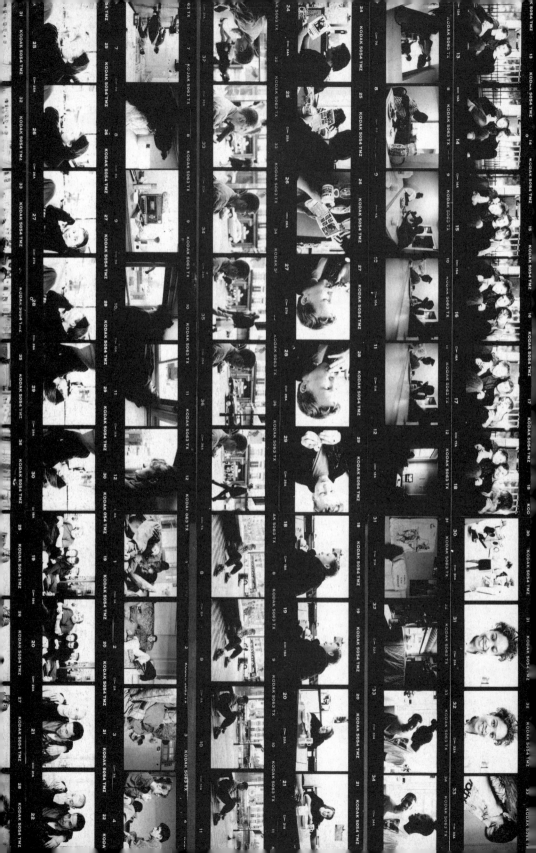